JERRY GOLDSMITH
MUSIC SCORING FOR
AMERICAN MOVIES

Mauricio Dupuis

Translated by
Cecilia Martini

DMG

Index

* * *

© Mauricio Gabriel Dupuis, 2014
http://www.lulu.com/spotlight/mauriciodupuis
http://mauriciogabrieldupuis.blogspot.it/

ISBN 978-88-909773-5-0
Second Edition, June 2014

PREFACE

Thank goodness we had Jerry's score.
He really saved us.
ROBERT WISE

Jerry Goldsmith, the American composer whose work spans from the 1950s to the beginning of the current century, can be considered one of the most significant names of musical creation applied to movies. A well-trained and cultured musician himself, he focused most of his work on movies, along with occasional incursions in orchestra and choral composition specifically conceived for concert halls. He also worked, at the beginning of his career especially, in radio and television, both of which turned out to be excellent training for his later work.

The present essay, among the composer's vast body of works, is centered on those connected to the American movie system. The focus will obviously be on Goldsmith's most meaningful scores, both in a strict musical sense and in relation to the movie they belong to, although each would be worthy of a lengthier and more specific analysis, such as those applied to musical theatre works. This book, however, will try to create a base for further studies.

The first and largest part – formed by chapters one to three – will concentrate on a few basic and recurring features of movie scoring: production context, relationships with directors and producers, orchestration and other practices of the composing "workshop"; we will then turn our attention to Goldsmith's specific case and finish the section with a brief excursus on the composer's career, which touched almost every movie genre. The second part – the fourth chapter – will cover his experience with the *Star Trek* saga, the work that turned him into an iconic composer. The book will end with a catalog of Goldsmith's body of work, including movies, television, radio, and other minor experiences.

As one of the main examples, together with John Williams, of the so-called *silver age*[1] of Hollywood music, this Californian composer's successful work in movies started in the second half of the 20th century, allowing him to collaborate with many of the most prolific directors of his time, and to be signed on by the most famous production studios. In this sense, Goldsmith represents a significant paradigm: a 20th century musician from a consistently classic tradition – albeit open-minded towards avant-garde movements – who made a profit from a seemingly thankless and secondary job, all the while managing to make his mark on music, as witnessed by the excellent record sales throughout his career.

Most musical examples in this book are taken from reproductions of sketches, handwritten by the composer or by his aides and donated by Goldsmith himself in 1997 to the Margaret Herrick Library of Los Angeles; library curator Warren M. Sherk catalogued these hard-to-access notebooks, which constitute a fundamental musicological starting point for the study of the composer.[2]

---

[1]   Such is the name of the American movie score era spanning from the end of the 1950s to the 1990s, as opposed to the *Golden Age* going from the first half of the 1930s to the beginning of the 1960s, the main representatives of which are Erich Wolfgang Korngold, Max Steiner, Miklós Rózsa, Franx Waxman, Alfred Newman, Bernard Herrmann and other, lesser composers.

[2]   The commercialization of orchestral movie scores is generally limited. The available scores are usually a miscellanea of (simplified) piano arrangements or single tracks in different versions (e.g. band arrangements). John Williams, who wrote scores for the *Star Wars* saga and for many of Steven Spielberg's movies, is a rare example of renowned composer who published his pieces as suites or single tracks in the original orchestra version.

1
A LIFE IN MOVIE PRODUCTIONS

Production context

Ever since expressive media such as radio, movies and, later, television made their appearance, the average 20th century composer often turned to the "applied" conception of musical composition; if, on the one hand, the subordination of music to a specific medium – in this case, movies – could be seen as an intellectual limitation, on the other hand it allowed for more opportunities of interacting with the current forms of artistic expression. Prior to the 1900s, the focus had been on such media as theatre and dancing, but the 20th century brought along a greater range of expressive possibilities. After the full development of sound in movies, during the 1930s, music and pictures started cooperating in earnest, forging a relationship that became a basic part of artistic and intellectual evolution in the 20th century.

While examining the movie production system – even when it is appropriate to use terms such as "art" and "strong individual expression" – we must bear in mind that the final product is never created by a single artisan, as it happens in other musical fields such as musical theatre or ballet. The composer, consequentially, does not enjoy the expressive freedom he would have when composing for himself or when being commissioned work from musical institutions or symphonic orchestras. Although the U.S. movie industry underwent drastic changes after the major studios' great crisis,[3] the various phases of movie production retained their basic "assembly line" approach: storyline, script, casting and direction, editing and musical composition. The same limitations applied to directors. In Europe, even today, the director is seen as the keystone of a cinematic work's personality. In the U.S., by contrast it is rare for the so-called *director's cut* of a movie

---

[3] A critical period starting in the 1960s and continuing into the following decade, exacerbated by the growing success of TV and of made-for-television movies.

5

to be released in theaters, and a studio-appointed producer usually has the last word on the editing process. As for scripts, they are often reviewed – or even distorted, especially as far as the ending is concerned – to match the requirements of a hypothetical audience. Even within this system's stifling conventions, however, it is clear that original voices can manage to surface and offer a significant contribution in both content and meaning.

Rather than to opera, movie scoring can be compared to the composition of incidental music for theatrical *pièces*, where the composer's space for individual expression is reduced in the extreme.[4] Movie scoring is generally regarded as mechanical work, and those who undertake it end up embodying the stereotype of eclecticism, becoming one-size-fits-all composers who oblige to follow explicit requests from a director or a producer; this usually means employing the common musical formulas of each genre, which the audience is trained to expect and recognize. In short, a composer who writes scores for pre-packaged works – be it in movies, radio, television or theatre – is almost always forced to avoid the use of bold musical language, with the paradoxical aim of finding a qualitative balance among the final material, or of simply matching the (often stereotypical) requests of his customers.

Whenever a high-level composer – such as Šostakovič, Prokof'ev, Walton or Vaughan-Williams, to name but a few – becomes involved in a second-rate movie,[5] the predictable result – given the musician's tal-

---

[4]   The past – before the invention of radio and cinema – is rife with examples. We might consider Mendelssohn and his version of Shakespeare's *Midsummer Night's Dream* (1826 and 1842), or Bizet's version of Daudet's *L'Arlésienne* (1872), just to mention two heavyweights.

[5]   It's hard to remember any instance when a relevant concert-repertoire composer would contribute to an important movie. Among the contributions by the aforementioned composers – the most active in the cinematic industry (Armenian composer Aram Khachaturyan may be added to the illustrious list) – it's worth remembering the "academic" example of *Aleksandr Nevskij* (1938), directed by Sergej Ejzenštejn and scored by Sergej Prokof'ev; the two artists would work together again a few years later on *Ivan the Terrible* (1944) – and *Hamlet* (1948), directed by Sir Laurence Olivier, with William Walton's music.

ent – is for the whole enterprise to be regarded as unsuccessful; at most we may be interested in not letting the music go to waste, forgetting the movies for which it was written.

Jerry Goldsmith's professional adventure evolves in an environment that is rather politically quiet if compared, for example, to the working conditions of the aforementioned Soviet composers, who were often summoned to work on propaganda movies.

Careful examination of Goldsmith's filmography reveals, in many cases, a complete discrepancy between some of his musical solutions and the movies they are meant for, the latter lacking, more often than not, in artistic expression. It is almost proverbial, among enthusiasts of this composer and of the applied cinematic genre in general, to consider Goldsmith a rare example of talent and technical ability frequently applied to projects lacking in ideas. And yet, it was precisely while working on the most old-fashioned genres – such as thrillers, action films, exotic or maritime adventures, war or fantasy movies – that the composer felt freer to experiment with his personal choices, employing peculiar timbre mixtures and a liberal use of dissonances, or even (sparingly and whenever it was necessarily) using electronics, all the better to exalt a specific theme – often pared down to a few notes or a simple rhythm. As for the composing technique itself, the author looked to a wide range of 20th century historic musicians, never shying away from new languages such as atonality. We are talking, therefore, about a modern composer who was attuned to the most advanced language techniques, open to tradition – due to his classical education – as well as to lighter techniques pertaining to "popular music" (albeit to a smaller extent,). In spite of his eclecticism– an almost inevitable trait, having to face such a consistent number of commissions –the composer was also able to acquire a recognizable form of style. Although his career started on the radio at the beginning of the 1950s, 1962 was the year of his first significant cinematic result: a contribution to the John Huston movie *Freud*. From then on, in the course of a forty-year career – ending with the score to Joe Dante's *Looney Tunes: Back in Action* (2003) – Goldsmith contributed to more than two hundred movies, to which we must add his (almost always secondary) television work.

Goldsmith seldom talked of the *poetics* of his movie work. Other composers have been more explicit in detailing their separate approach to concert music and movie scoring.[6] A few of them even hold their cinematic work in higher esteem – namely, Bernard Herrmann and Miklós Rózsa, two of Goldsmith's mentors, who left their mark in the composer's life, especially at the beginning of his career.

Herrmann (1911-75),[7] born in New York and known for his work with both Orson Welles and Alfred Hitchcock, had a resolute and uncompromising personality, and considered himself an all-accomplished composer, engaging in movies as much as in any other expressive medium (he also dabbled in opera and concert music). Consequentially, even when working on movies, he demanded complete freedom.

Rózsa (1907-95), a Hungarian who emigrated to England first and then to the U.S., where he became a famous score composer for big-budget historical movies (*Ben-Hur, El Cid, King of Kings*, to name but a few), stated in his autobiography that the number of concert compositions he wrote did not show a significant gap in quality and language when compared to those he did for the movies – for a total of about a hundred titles. While Herrmann experimented with rhythm, Rózsa (much like Rachmaninov) was a 20th century Romantic composer. This meant he preferred to use a less advanced musical language, keeping his work within the tonal and modal without ever reaching dodeca-

---

[6] Among them is Ennio Morricone. In addition to Sergio Miceli's essay on Ennio Morricone (SERGIO MICELI, *Morricone, la musica, il cinema*, Milan-Modena, Ricordi-Mucchi, 1994), another contribution on Morricone's role as a "two-faced deity" dividing himself between movies and concert halls is ROBERTO SCOLLO's *Morricone uno e due*, in ENZO KERMOL and MARISELDA TESSAROLO (ed.), *La musica del cinema*, Rome, Bulzoni, 1996, p.161-176.

[7] Herrmann is currently enjoying considerable critical and musicological attention. Among the first comprehensive analytical studies is the following work on his score for *Vertigo*: DAVID COOPER, *Bernard Herrmann's Vertigo - A Film Score Handbook*, Wesport/London, Greenwood Press, 2001. The same series, among others, includes a study by Kate Daubney on Max Steiner's *Now, Voyager* (1942).

phony (twelve-tone technique), which he did not hold in very high esteem. Save for a few exceptions, composers who are more open to avant-garde – even when only moderately advanced, from a musicological point of view – often feel less at ease with the more "communicative" and tonally clear music usually required for a movie.

Goldsmith's compositions outside of movie scoring were few and far between, mainly commissioned by symphonic and theatrical institutions: between 1969 and 1972 he created the *Christus Apollo* cantata (1969, lyrics by Ray Bradbury), the *Music for Orchestra* orchestral composition (1971), and the *Othello* ballet (1972). After a lapse of several years it was time for *Fireworks*, a piece commissioned by the Los Angeles Philharmonic in celebration of its hometown (1999).[8] Goldsmith's colleague John Williams, on the other hand, maintained a prolific concert production since the 1970s; the commercial success enjoyed by some of his music allowed him to concentrate only on specific cinematic projects, while devoting himself to concerts and original compositions, especially for well-known concert musicians.

After acting as conductor (with few exceptions) during the recordings of his own scores, Goldsmith took on the same role in concert halls, though less assiduously, especially in the second half of the 1980s. The request for live exhibitions of his movie *suites* grew in time, causing him to produce a few records as mementos. Fewer are the instances of him directing someone else's music. During the 1990s he devoted himself to rediscovering and celebrating another one of his mentors, Russian-American Alex North (1910-91), to whom he was bound by deep friendship as well as professional esteem. To Goldsmith, together with the National Philharmonic Orchestra, we owe the first execution of the music composed by North for Stanley Kubrick's science-fiction masterpiece *2001: A Space Odyssey* (1968), which the director famously

---

[8] The complete title being *Fireworks- A Celebration of Los Angeles*. While this is a quite an "approachable" piece, though endowed with Goldsmith's typical lively rhythm, the composer's works from the 1970s (especially *Music for Orchestra* and *Christus Apollo*) are undertaken with the use of a more overtly modern language.

rejected; the long-forgotten score was later brought to light and recorded by an independent label specializing in movie soundtracks.[9]

The practice of conducting is very common among movie composers, though most of them only conduct their own music. Herrmann and Williams, however, have been known to conduct music by other composers, even when it pertained to the traditional symphonic repertoire. Herrmann was among the first musicians to conduct Charles Ives' music when the latter was still relatively unknown. Herrmann, an accomplished musician himself, also conducted and recorded music by Walton, Vaughan-Williams, Milhaud and Satie, among others. Williams is remembered for his interpretation of Aaron Copland's *The Red Pony* and Gustav Holst's *The Planets*, a score that greatly influenced his own adventure in science fiction par excellence, *Star Wars*.

Given the scarcity of studies on cinematic music – and especially on a figure as significant in this realm as Goldsmith's – it is often necessary to "make do" with the few mentions of his work in specialized magazines, as well as with the composer's sporadic statements in interviews or – more recently – in audio commentaries to his movies, reissued on DVD. Despite such scarcity, it is worth mentioning this short but interesting passage:

> Of the few composers with talent and genius who are extremely active in scoring films today, Jerry Goldsmith must be ranked as one of the most significant contributors in the 1960s and 1970s to the art of film scoring. Goldsmith's creative imagination seems almost boundless, a fact made even surprising by the Mozartian swiftness with which he produces scores of dramatic significance. His subtle dramatic sense is equaled by only a handful of his colleagues. Like any fine film composer, Goldsmith is aware of the overriding importance of "spotting" music for a film.[10]

The following study by Roy Prendergast – a rare example of musi-

9   Published by Varèse Sarabande, Vsd-5400, 1993.

10 Roy M. Prendergast, *Film Music: a Neglected Art*, New York/ London, W.W. Norton, 1992[2], p.158. The scholar's statements must be referred to the time of the book's first edition (1977), though they can be applied to the following period as well.

cological essay dealing with movie scoring history, aesthetics and technologies – reports the following, even more significant, statement from Goldsmith:

> Goldsmith sees his score "as a total piece and not just as a series of sequences. The score is a piece of music. Everything is developed from one piece of material. The most important thing to me is that everything develops out of the initial organic material. All my scores work that way. If the music has no form, no foundation – no basis from where it came then why is it there in the first place?"[11]

Though his composing activity occurred in close connection to movies, and his music reached a high level of functionality, Goldsmith still believed his scores had their own internal structure and, consequentially, a life of their own. He worked within the great American movie studios'[12] production system. His spirit of adaptation was remarkable, as proven by the fact that almost all major Studios benefited from his work. His collaboration with movie production studios allows us to trace some of the most significant phases of his career.

From his debut in movies in 1957 up until 1962, Goldsmith seldom created scores for the silver screen, as he was consistently busy with television work (being under contract with CBS from 1950 to 1960). In 1962 Alfred Newman – one of the most significant figures in Hollywood music and the director of 20th Century-Fox's music department – helped Goldsmith write two of his first relevant scores: *Freud* and *Lonely Are the Brave*, both from the same year. During his first five years of movie work, from 1957 to 1962, the composer wrote ten scores: three for Universal and two for Columbia, followed by United Artists, Warner Bros and MGM (one for each), as well as a British-produced documentary and a TV movie that was used as a series pilot.

---

[11] *Ibid.*, p.158-159.

[12] *Studios* are traditionally divided into *Majors* (RKO, Warner, MGM, 20th Century-Fox, Paramount), medium (Columbia and Universal), Disney and minor ones, such as Republic. Hence the term *studio-system*, used to define the movie industry of the Los Angeles area.

The year 1963 marked the beginning of a long and crucial phase in Goldsmith's career, which continued until 1980 for a total of ninety-nine works. Though still under contract with Fox (forty productions, including a made-for-television movie), he was able to work for other studios: MGM (fifteen productions, including TV co-productions with ABC and CBS), Paramount (ten productions, the *Star Trek* saga among them), Columbia (seven productions, including four TV movies, one of which was co-produced by ABC), Warner Bros (six productions, including two co-productions with CBS and one with Allied), Universal (five productions, including one TV movie co-produced by NBC), United Artists (three productions), AVCO (two productions), Allied (two productions, one of them co-produced by Warner), Disney, NGP, First Asian and AIP (one production each).

The 1970s saw a growth in made-for-television movies produced by CBS (eight, including two co-produced by Warner), ABC (five) and NBC (one, co-produced by Universal). Out of eighty strictly cinematic works, therefore, a little less than half (thirty-nine) were produced by 20th Century-Fox. During that same period, especially between 1970 and 1977, Goldsmith's role as a composer for made-for-television movies (commissioned by CBS, ABC and NBC) overlapped the final stretch in his work on TV shows, for a total of nineteen scores in seven years; to these we must add the tail end represented by *Masada: the Heroic Fortress* (1981; directed by Boris Sagal; an over six-hour-long mini-series), which stands as his last complete television work.

In 1981 Goldsmith called off his longtime collaboration with Fox in order to become a freelance composer. This, with the added factor of the major studios' crises and the growing assertion of multinational companies, coincided with the appearance of newly-constituted studios such as Tristar (which would later merge with Columbia), Cannon, Orion, Embassy, Carolco and Dreamworks. Some of them would be short-lived, others, though young, would prove very active. During this final 20-year-plus span (reaching the start of the 21st century), Goldsmith wrote more than ninety scores, though he would never forge another stable work relationship like the one he had once had with Fox.

Overall it was the most traditional studios that still required his contribution, even though their managing structure had changed: Columbia-TriStar (fifteen, including a rejected score), Universal (fourteen, including a rejected score and two co-productions, the first one with 20th Century-Fox and the second one with Dreamworks, as well as the *Masada* TV-movie), Warner (twelve), Paramount (eleven, including a rejected score), MGM (nine, one of which was rejected); 20th Century-Fox (eight, including two rejected scores, a co-production with Universal and another with AIP); Disney (eight, including the company's associates Touchstone and Buena Vista); and finally, Orion (three), Dreamworks (three, including one co-produced by Universal), Cannon (two), and Carolco, Hemdale, Pathé, Embassy, Aband, ITC, Kings Road, New World, AIP (one each).

* * *

Career

Jerrald King Goldsmith (hence the nickname Jerry)[13] was born in Pasadena, California, on February 10, 1929, a crucial year for the U.S. in general and for movie-making in particular, with the creation of the first talking pictures. Many composers and artisans, as well as producers, directors and actors from the generation that preceded Goldsmith's in Hollywood (the so-called *golden age* of American movies) had been European: Erich Wolfgang Korngold (1897-1957), Max Steiner (1888-1971), Franz Waxman (1906-67), and the aforementioned Hungarian Miklós Rózsa, who, together with U.S. native Alfred Newman, are to be considered the five most important composers working during the early decades of the *talkies*.[14] Korngold and Waxman – Steiner

---

[13] He also used some pen-names, especially Michael J. Hennagin, at the beginning of his career.

[14] To these we must add the aforementioned Bernard Herrmann, who, despite being born in 1911, was very successful during the 1970s *Silver Age*, working in movies by De Palma and Scorsese (as well as Truffaut).

13

had arrived earlier, – like many of their better-known colleagues (Schönberg in particular) had been forced to emigrate from Europe by the ominous racial laws enforced by the Nazi regime, long before the start of WWII. They managed to continue working in the U.S. after countries such as Austria, Germany and Poland (another composer worth remembering is Poland-born Bronislau Kaper) had forbidden them to do so.

Goldsmith can be considered one of the first California-born leading musicians of the State's studio system (Alfred Newman, a unique case among the "great pioneers" had been from Connecticut). He was luckier than his older colleagues in the sense that, for historical reasons, he did not experience the existential problems of the other intellectuals who shared his Jewish cultural roots. He, on the other hand, would later experience the whole Cold War phase, which would greatly influence some of the movies he scored.

He started studying music in his teens; during the 1940s he studied piano with pianist and composer Jakob Gimpel (1906-89), himself a pupil of Alban Berg's, as well as learning theory and composition from another distinguished expatriate, Florentine Mario Castelnuovo-Tedesco (1895-1968), who in turn had studied with Ildebrando Pizzetti and had been Alfredo Casella's protégé. Later on, Goldsmith also studied with a prominent figure of California's star-studded composing scene, the aforementioned Rózsa, whom he met at University of Southern California after 1948. At the Los Angeles City College he studied with Eric Zeisl (1905-59) and especially with Ernst Krenek (1900-91). The latter's exceptional teachings proved more successful than others (such as those of Castelnuovo-Tedesco and Zeisl, both closer to the late-19th century traditional musical language) in drawing Goldsmith to the use of the twelve-tone technique. Castelnuovo-Tedesco, at any rate, had little influence on such a young student; Goldsmith kept closer ties with Gimpel, his childhood teacher, who would later contribute, as a pianist, to a seminal work of the composer's musical and cinematic career: *Planet of the Apes* (1968).

Before delving further into Goldsmith's career, it is useful to remember a brief statement he gave about the years of his education and their relation to his later work:

> My teacher was myself. I studied composition, theory, harmony and counterpoint with teachers, but coming in film scoring you teach yourself. You can't really teach it! I was fortunate... I worked in the '50s for five years on live television: you screwed up, came back next week and again had another attempt at it.[15]

He started his professional life as a copyist for CBS, in 1950.[16] In the course of the decade he worked with some extremely accomplished composers, writing arrangements and preparing orchestrations for radio and television. During this time he started composing his first – not very original – scores for television series. Some of them were significant in marking a certain approach to a peculiar genre – western and science fiction especially – which the author would then try to develop in the same kind of movies, as a personal way of managing his composing resources. While working for CBS, he had the chance to appreciate the personality and work of Bernard Herrmann, a composer whose musical language in scores, at the time, was the most cutting-edge on the U.S. movie scene. Goldsmith regarded Herrmann as a master of style, and we can actually trace a connection between the two, as they both put emphasis on less-than-predictable musical parameters such as timbre and rhythm. In this sense we might find a direct, ideal stylistic heritage, for different reasons, between Korngold and Williams, whose music is generally regarded as more "open". Personal relations between Herrmann and Goldsmith, however, were not very friendly, especially due to the former's touchy personality. Speaking of which,

---

[15] Transcription of the commentary to *Hollow Man* (2000), in the Columbia Pictures DVD, chapter 10.

[16] TONY THOMAS, *Music for the Movies*, Los Angeles, Silman-James, 1997 (second edition) p.284. Tony Thomas (1927-1997), "historical memory" of Hollywood movie scores, was among the first to publish a collection of anecdotes about great Hollywood composers – in 1973 – drawing inspiration mainly from his relationship to the recording and movie industries.

we can relate an incident which, unfortunately, left its mark on their relationship. It is reported by Steven C. Smith:

> At the same time, a less temperamental composer [Goldsmith, a/n] sixteen years Herrmann's junior was building a reputation in CBS radio and television. After a brief internship in the network's music library, Jerry Goldsmith had become one of CBS's most imaginative and economical musicians. (For his first score, for the series 'Romance' (...) he was paid an all-inclusive $50). Goldsmith had watched Herrmann conduct 'Crime Classics' programs and, until 1956, had idolized him. But Goldsmith's success – and a radio programming error – led to a recurrence of Herrmann's now-familiar pattern of support followed by suspicion. "I was doing a series at the time called 'Studio One' ", Goldsmith said, "we would score the show and then they would do a minute teaser or trailer of the next week's show. (...) There was never time to write music and play it. Unfortunately this week they picked a piece of Bernie's music that had been in the library and they used it as the underscoring for the trailer. Now the credits came up – 'Music composed and conducted by Jerry Goldsmith'. Well... he was going to sue everybody. He went around the studio demanding all sorts of incredible things. "There's Goldsmith! He's stealing my music!" and naturally I tried explaining to him... Well, the more you explained it, it only exasperated the situation. So from that point on that was the end of our relationship."[17]

It is not easy to understand the behavior of an otherwise intelligent artist such as Herrmann, who did not seem to fully comprehend the technicalities of a radio and television musician's daily work. One had to write and record quickly, often re-arranging pre-existing musical pieces. Herrmann had long been active in these two sectors: starting in

---

[17] STEVEN C. SMITH, *A Heart at Fire's Center- The Life and Works of Bernard Herrmann*, Berkeley, Los Angeles, London, University of California Press, 1991. The passage is taken from the 2002 paperback edition, p.204. Smith relates Goldsmith's tale as it appeared in an interview on "Filmmusic Notebook" No.2 (1977), p.20. Such a vehement reaction from the composer can only be justified with an almost visceral attachment his own compositions, even the less inspired ones; his inability to comprehend the reason for the misunderstanding is the only unsavory element in the incident.

the mid-'30s he had the chance to work with Orson Welles, an experience that prepared both artists for their important collaborations of the early '40s (*Citizen Kane*, *The Magnificent Ambersons*).

Personal relations aside, the two composers' cinematic works, though dissimilar, share an ideal pursuit of the best rhythmic behavior and the most congenial (sometimes even unorthodox) timbric palette. Goldsmith's radio experience saw him working on series such as *Suspense*, *The CBS Radio Workshop*, *Juvenile Court*, *Frontier Gentleman*, *Romance* (he also wrote the opening credits music for *Juvenile Court* and *Frontier Gentleman*). His television work, starting roughly at the same time as his work in radio, was substantial and long-standing. The composer's exclusive work in movies started only in 1975.[18] The '50s saw him working almost exclusively on various CBS series: *Studio One* (on air from 1948 to 1958; music written for twelve episodes), *General Electric Theatre* (1953\1962, four episodes),[19] *The Line Up* (1954\1960, two episodes and main theme), *Climax* (1954\1958; eleven episodes), *Playhouse 90* (1956\1960; ten episodes). These series showed the typical structure of the era – anthology clips often introduced by a live studio guest. Few traces remain of such works, save for a mention of the episodes Goldsmith participated in; they were pure entertainment, which gave him, as a young musician, the chance to test the economics of musical media, to best adapt to what he was provided with – often no more than a small orchestra – and deal with tight-on-time writing and recording processes.

Those were the years of the first fictional TV show productions, the three main veins being western, judicial/crime and horror-tinged science fiction. Goldsmith devoted himself to these genres with nary a trace of snobbery. One of his first significant experiences, dating from

---

[18] With the exception of the occasional TV movie (*Masada*, 1981), Goldsmith's work on TV series would never be systematical again: only in 1986 did he agree to write music for an episode of *Amazing Stories* and, during the course of the '90s, he wrote the main themes for *H.e.l.p.* (1990) and *Star Trek-Voyager* (1995).

[19] Whenever only two dates are mentioned, they are to be considered as the start and the ending of a TV show.

1959, was connected to two episodes from the third season of *Perry Mason*. Then came the western series, prominently featured among television productions all through the 1960s: three episodes of *Gunsmoke* in 1960 (on air from 1955 to 1975 for a grand total of twenty seasons), two episodes of *Have Gun, Will Travel* (on air from 1957 to 1963), two more episodes of *Gunsmoke* in 1961 (another one in 1966 would bring Goldsmith's contribution to this long-running series to a close) and one episode of *Rawhide* (1959\68). He then contributed to *Wagon Train* (1957\66), *Wanted Dead or Alive* (1958\61), *Ben Casey* (1961\66), *Black Saddle* (1959\62; two episodes), *The Loner* (1965; two episodes and main theme), and *The Legend of Jesse James* (1965). To these we must add the author's brief experience with the wartime serial *Jericho* (1966).

The 1970s brought a renewal of his contracts with western TV series, though these were starting to mix with different genres, e.g. family drama; such was the case with *The Waltons* (on air between 1972 and 1981; in 1972, Goldsmith scored six episodes of this show as well as its opening credits)[20], as well as lesser-known ones. As for crime series, it is worth mentioning his contribution to *Barnaby Jones* (1973/80), for which he scored the opening credits and pilot episode. This show, dating from the mid-'70s, would mark the end of Goldsmith's work on TV serials; from then on he would only contribute to them on occasion.

Going back a few years, it is more interesting to examine the composer's work on science-fiction, fantasy or mystery shows. Between 1960 and 1961 Goldsmith offered substantial contribution to two series: a more traditional one, *Thriller* (fifteen episodes between 1960 and 1961, plus two where his music was used again), a short-lived NBC series introduced by cult actor Boris Karloff; and a more innovative one, *The Twilight Zone*, created by Rod Serling,[21] originally on air from

---

[20] The TV show was based on a made-for-TV movie for which Goldsmith had written music in 1971, Fielder Cook's *The Homecoming- A Christmas Story*.

[21] On air for five seasons and a total of 156 episodes. In 1983, Steven Spielberg and three more directors (John Landis, Joe Dante and George Miller) created a movie version of the show, an homage to a cultural phenomenon that had proved so fundamental to American and international imagination. The whole score for *Twilight Zone- The Movie* was written by Goldsmith.

1959 to 1964. The latter is significant for its music, as well as for its base concept: along with Goldsmith, it boasts contributions by some of the top movie scoring names of the time: Bernard Herrmann, Leonard Rosenman, Fred Steiner, and Franz Waxman; the opening-credits theme that would soon become the series' trademark was written by Marius Constant. Goldsmith's contribution to this series was focused on the first two seasons – from 1960 to 1961 – for a total of seven episodes. Unlike most of his TV production, such contributions would prove quite successful in terms of record sales, although the overall quality of his work never reached the structural complexity of his later movie scores. In 1964 Goldsmith took on a leading role in contributing to another well-known U.S. series, *The Man from U.N.C.L.E.*, a bizarre mixture of comedy, adventure and spy fiction: Goldsmith only worked on the first of the show's five seasons (105 episodes on air from 1964 to 1968). The composer created music for three episodes, including the series pilot; some of his existing music was reproduced in thirteen more episodes; he also wrote the theme for the opening credits, which became so famous he would later perform it during concert *suites* devoted to his TV work.

The crime-detective genre, which Goldsmith fleetingly touched in 1959 with *Perry Mason* and to which he later returned with *Hawkins* (1974; Goldsmith, having composed the score for the 1973 movie *Hawkins on Murder*, was hired to write the theme music for the show's opening credits) proved less fortunate: the short-lived 20th Century-Fox pilot for *Nick Quarry* (1968), followed by *Room 222* (after premiering in 1969, it only lasted for a handful of episodes), *Police Story* (1973\80; Goldsmith worked on the original *The Police Story* movie and wrote music for seven episodes of its spin-off series' first season) and *Archer* (1975; music for one of the series' six episodes). He briefly dabbled in drama (a secondary genre even in his movie production) with *Dr. Kildare* (1961\66), for which he wrote the opening credits music in 1961; *Anna and the King* (just a few episodes in 1972)[22] and music

---

22 The series' plot was based on the 1946 movie *Anna and the King of Siam* (directed by John Cromwell, with music by Bernard Herrmann) as well as the 1956 movie musical *The King and I*, directed by Walter Lang, based in turn on the musical comedy

for the movie version of *Medical Story* (1975). He also contributed to lesser, long-forgotten works: in 1972 he scored *When Widows Weep*, a special revival episode of *Lights Out*, a series on air from 1946 to 1972; in 1974 he worked on *Police Woman*, a spin-off crime show based on *Police Story*. After 1975 his contribution to television, at least as far as series were concerned, came to an end: this silence would later be broken, after the *Amazing Stories* event, by the main themes for two more series: *H.e.l.p.* and *Star Trek-Voyager*,[23] a *Star Trek* tie-in that would serve as a crucial contribution to the *Star Trek* movie.

The start of the composer's movie adventure occurred in conjunction with his most intense period of television experience, spanning from the end of the '50s to the beginning of the following decade. Goldsmith had first approached this "higher" medium in 1952, by writing additional music for Roy Ward Baker's movie *Don't Bother to Knock*, officially scored by Lionel Newman (1916-89); the latter, initially one of Goldsmith's mentors, would later conduct many of his scores (*The Sand Pebbles*, *Bandolero!*, the *The Omen* trilogy, *Alien*). Five years later, Goldsmith worked alone on his first movie score: *Black Patch* (1957; directed by Allen H. Miller), a mediocre Warner Brothers western. Up until 1962, Goldsmith's work in movies had been scarce and irrelevant – five contributions between 1957 and 1961 – with the exception of 1960's *Studs Lonigan*, which can be considered better than average.

The year 1962 marked a turning point, as Goldsmith found himself working with such directors as Robert Mulligan and John Huston. The three resulting scores, all produced by Universal, provided the composer with considerable exposure: *Freud* (directed by Huston and starring Montgomery Clift as the father of psychoanalysis), *Lonely Are the Brave* (directed by David Miller; a crepuscular western written by Dalton Trumbo and starring Kirk Douglas) and *The Spiral Road* (Mulligan's medical drama starring Rock Hudson).

As a testament to the consideration that Goldsmith's music was

---

written by Richard Rodgers and Oscar Hammerstein II.

[23] In other *Star Trek* TV movies and series, as well as in movies from the *Star Trek* saga, Goldsmith's music is constantly referenced or rearranged by other composers.

starting to receive, we relate an episode from this time, once again involving Bernard Herrmann. While assisting to the *Lonely Are the Brave* recording session, Herrmann advised Goldsmith not to waste such excellent music on a movie:

> Relations between the two composers had never been good (largely due, it seems, to a misunderstanding on Herrmann's part) nor were they improved when Goldsmith, doing one of his first major pictures for Universal [*Lonely Are the Brave*, 1962, *a/n*], was publicly excoriated by Herrmann for working with an orchestrator (a practice Herrmann abhorred). Then, without a word of warning, Herrmann appeared on the sound-stage while a recording session for that film was in progress. "But he did walk in at a very opportune moment", recalls Goldsmith, "it happened to be the best piece of music in the score and was quite exciting. And [Herrmann] said: "Don't use that music – it's too damn good for the picture! You save it, it's too damn good for the picture!". The point is that in spite of all his animosities, prejudices and idiosyncrasies he was a musician to the core, his musical instincts could not be denied and in that area he could not help but be honest." [24]

As Palmer himself underlines at the end of the aforementioned passage, even though Herrmann's convictions drove him to criticize anything he did not consider musically *pure* (especially the *total* composition of a musical piece),[25] he could not deny his aesthetic approval to his colleague's final musical result. Goldsmith, on the other hand, rarely showed a similar haughtiness towards the people he accepted to work with, which only proved how committed he was to his work. Whenever he could, in fact, he tried to enrich it and push it towards creative progress. In the course of his career he used below-standard movie commissions (thrillers, horrors, lower-rate adventure movies) as a training ground to experiment with less conventional solutions, while at the same time helping the movie be more successful than it otherwise might have been. Despite being part of a production "ma-

---

[24] CHRISTOPHER PALMER, *The Composer in Hollywood*, Marion Boyars, London, New York, 1990, p.237. The incident is also related by SMITH, in *A Heart at Fire's Center*, op.cit.

[25] Orchestration included: as for this issue, see below.

chine" he strived to keep his personal touch, even when writing on commission or intervening in a movie's final stages (e.g. preliminary or final editing), by experimenting with unusual solutions – especially in timbre – and imposing the musical language he considered most in tune with the proposed result.

His first movie efforts – with the possible exception of *Freud* – appear to lack in courage, as they are channeled to the use of well-established genre stereotypes from the previous twenty years; the composer, moreover, was fresh out of a decade of background work at CBS, which pushed him to conform to the dictates of common practice. It would not be fair to compare his beginnings to the memorable debut of the aforementioned Herrmann, on Orson Welles' 1941 *Citizen Kane*, especially as the two composers' professional situations appear to be completely different: Herrmann avoided gaining substantial occupation in movies – composing only fifty scores in the course of thirty-five years (Goldsmith, in comparison, wrote a grand total of about two hundred in forty years)[26] focusing instead on the composition of concert pieces and a theatrical opera (*Wuthering Heights*, based on the novel by Emily Brontë), plus a symphonic cantata inspired by Melville's *Moby Dick*. In spite of his cautious beginnings, Goldsmith managed to provide *Freud* with a musical language that was closer to the avant-gardes, making him one of the most cutting-edge American movie composers of his time. From 1963 onwards he was offered a lot of work (mainly due to his 1962 movie hits) which he accepted without much discrimination. He had the chance of working with John Huston again on *The List of Adrian Messenger*.[27] Between 1963 and 1964 his work, ranging from spy-comedy hybrids to war dramas, was not very significant,

---

[26] Not counting the two composers' frequent work on TV and radio series.

[27] Less demanding than *Freud*, this movie is little more than a fun exercise in the style of thrillers. Its peculiarity lies in the many famous actors (Robert Mitchum, Burt Lancaster, Frank Sinatra, Tony Curtis) made unrecognizable by makeup and starring in secondary roles; Kirk Douglas is the movie's main star as the murderer, while George C. Scott plays the policeman looking for him. From that moment on, Scott frequently appeared in movies scored by Goldsmith, most notably *Patton* (1970) and *Islands in the Stream* (1977).

though he did manage to create his first relevant western score, *Rio Conchos* (1964; directed by Gordon Douglas). He often returned to this particular genre, writing several scores during the following years.

In spite of his fame and his continuous work within the "system", Goldsmith did not receive many official awards, as opposed to his contemporary John Williams who, thanks to his easier approach to musical communication and his association with more successful movies, certainly had a better chance of spreading his music outside of the industry.[28] The difficulty of listening to Goldsmith's works when deprived of their cinematic component is often compared (with a few, less complex exceptions) to the problems associated with avant-garde pieces, where the traditional concept of melody gives way to other references – timbre, unusual instrumental mixes and harmony. The latter is often full of dissonance and purposefully ambiguous, although it always reaches the desired acoustic result. The composer's most significant experimentations occurred between the end of the '60s and the beginning of the '80s, a time considered "bad" for movie scores, as the general preference veered towards more accessible music; this was meant to favor commercial exploitation, especially through various kinds of songs (from pop, to rock to disco, according to current trends). Goldsmith himself, like many of his European colleagues such as Ennio Morricone, was more than once forced to write self-sustaining songs. In Goldsmith's case the songs, often tinged with nostalgia, were almost exclusively connected to westerns, with one notable exception. We are referring to *The Omen*, a thriller/horror whose theme song *The Piper Dreams* was based on an existing orchestra motif; the song appeared as the movie's only conventional recurring theme, aiming to underscore the initial, deceiving tranquility of the story, centered on the family of an American ambassador (Gregory Peck) in London. The composer, however, was never very inclined to write songs to be used for the re-

---

[28]   Goldsmith's only Academy Award dates back to 1976 for *The Omen* (directed by Richard Donner). However, the Academy of Motion Pictures Arts and Sciences often nominated Goldsmith, even for some of his less-than-traditional movie scores (such as *Planet of the Apes*).

cord industry's benefit: in this case, the melody had been written with a dramatic function, and had later evolved into a song due to an external contribution.

Among the various genres Goldsmith worked on, the scores written for science fiction, adventure and thriller pictures are to be considered his best, while the composer was less familiar with comedy and drama (which, at any rate, only occasionally appear in his filmography). The '80s and '90s brought him a consistent number of requests, although the first cracks in demand were starting to appear, and Goldsmith's scores were sometimes rejected (see appendix). In 1992, for example, Goldsmith was dismissed twice: these events foreshadowed the first real crisis in his career, although in the same year he managed to obtain a significant result with Paul Verhoeven's *Basic Instinct*. In the last ten years of his life, the composer wrote scores for some less-than-successful movies, with a few memorable exceptions: *First Knight* (1995; directed by Jerry Zucker), *L.A. Confidential* (1997; Curtis Hanson) and *Hollow Man* (2000; Verhoeven). Other scores (mainly for adventure movies) can at best be considered an echo of his past glories, albeit created with high composing skill: in this sense, they represent the birth of a distinctive "Goldsmith style". Having fallen seriously ill in 2002, the composer was forced to stay away from work for about a year. He returned to public life in the role of conductor, though on fewer occasions than before.[29] His last cinematic efforts, released in 2003, were the scores for the adventure movie *Timeline* (directed by Richard Donner and based on a Michael Crichton novel), which was later rejected by the production team,[30] and for the semi-animated *Looney Tunes: Back in Action* (directed by Joe Dante). While still involved in a few projects, Goldsmith died at age 75 on the night of July 21st, 2004, in Beverly Hills.

---

[29] On February 17, 2004 the London Symphony Orchestra celebrated Goldsmith's 75th birthday with a special program conducted by Dutch maestro Dirk Brossé, a last-minute replacement to Goldsmith himself, on account of the composer's deteriorating state of health.

[30] Although it never appeared in the movie, this score was published by the Varèse Sarabande recording label.

2
CREATIVE PROCESS

Being an extremely accomplished composer, Goldsmith managed, during the course of his career, to explore different cinematic routes; he tackled almost every genre the production studios imposed on him, whether it was suited to his personal traits or not. Upon examining the list of directors he worked with, a lack of *authors* in the European sense (directors, that is to say, who also write stories and scripts for the screen) is immediately apparent. Unlike in European cinema, *movie authors* are fairly rare in the U.S. in general and in Hollywood in particular; brilliant directors, in fact, have frequently had a hard time working in the (often mediocre) current industry – Orson Welles, for one, faced huge production difficulties following his first two movies, and for a long time he was forced to shoot his films abroad and to use makeshift equipment, while keeping up his work as an actor in medium- and low-grade movies, both in the U.S. and abroad. In the U.S. movie system, therefore, directors are often little more than honest artisans or, at best, shapers of somebody else's ideas. The so-called "genre" movies are based on a repetition of plots, shooting techniques and stereotypes. Movies that do not conform to a canon or that, even when pertaining to a specific genre, manage to overcome its stereotypes (a poignant example is given by so-called "Death of the Old West" films such as *The Wild Bunch*, 1969, and *Unforgiven*, 1992), are usually considered cinematic masterpieces.

For most of his movie work, Goldsmith mainly contributed to genre movies, with just a few memorable exceptions in his vast filmography. Thanks to his experienced technique, however, he managed to give his best when faced with aesthetic imperfection. Like most movie composers he worked on a tight schedule, and there is little doubt that his high workmanship allowed him to give directors the results they expected. The symbiosis between directors and composers which is more strongly (and, in some cases, systematically) felt in Europe is seldom found in the States. As a consequence, rather than being a meeting of minds, movies are a teamwork where the last to arrive – usually the composer – has the sole task of "filling in" or enhancing a picture's weaker points, always keeping editing in mind and striving not to be too invasive. The composer himself observed, about this:

> I think that we are trying to be a little more selective about where the music goes in a film (...). My preference is that music be used as sparingly as possible. I feel that if there is a constant use of music, or too much music, it will eventually vitiate the needed moments. The music becomes like white sound. It's like living in an area that has a high degree of density of traffic noises. Your ear eventually tunes out those frequencies.[31]

Restraint, therefore, was one of Goldsmith's main principles: music must only be present when absolutely necessary. Truth be told, he often followed the exact opposite approach: a striking example is given by *Alien*'s (1979) final sequence, for which the composer had initially written a very forceful, percussive and violent score; later, during the editing phase, the introduction of other pieces allowed more space to the visual aspect of the movie and produced very a different final result. Goldsmith's opinion, however, was that:

> The Europeans started a trend in films where it got to be rather *chic* to use no music at all in films. This idea has more or less climaxed in the films of Peter Bogdanovich, which have no formal scores.[32]

This comment, in addition to being a sort of defense of his profession, was undoubtedly connected to Goldsmith's aesthetic, and to his belief that music was a fundamental part of a movie. The absence of music is as unpopular, among movie composers, as the often misleading and out-of context use of classical repertoire pieces. An excessive musical presence, in principle, contradicted the composer's poetics. The above opinion was probably recorded in the '70s, when the presence of music in movies was overall limited; in more recent times, however, some

---

[31]   PRENDERGAST, *Film Music*, p.158.
[32]   *Ibid*.

movies scored by Goldsmith showed a rather relevant musical presence; and, although this cannot be considered a rule, movie productions from the second half of the '80s required a more significant opulence in music.

* * *

Orchestrations

Despite being one of the essential components of musical writing, orchestration or instrumentation is still considered somewhat of a mystery in the composing methods of the movie industry in general and the American one in particular. Anyone who is familiar with musical tradition considers this component to be the prerogative of composers, who also deal with harmony, rhythm etc. The possibility of somebody else working on it is usually not considered.

Even some of the most famous composers feel sometimes inadequate when writing for orchestras, or are considered to be lacking in this phase of musical construction. For this and other reasons, especially aesthetic ones, composers often turn to smaller ensembles (solo instruments or chamber music ensembles) instead of bigger ones. One famous example is represented by Fryderyk Chopin; the reactions to his rare experiments outside of piano composition (two concerts for piano and orchestra which, together with two chamber music works, form a minor part of his production) cast a doubt on the renowned composer's orchestral capacities. Robert Schumann's choices on this fundamental component of musical writing were often criticized as well, especially by famous conductors.[33] Another significant example is given by first-rate composers such as Modest Musorgskij and Anton Bruckner, who spent their whole lives being criticized for this and other supposed musical shortcomings. Aside from such famous (and overall isolated) examples, the composer was normally thought of – start-

---

[33] A striking example was the pretension, from famous composer-conductor Gustav Mahler, to "improve" Schumann's four symphonies.

27

ing from the baroque period, when musical writing became more targeted towards orchestras and chamber music ensembles than towards vocal – as someone who could face any genre and any ensemble, without the authorship of his timbric choices ever being questioned.

Among movie composers, however, this aspect of composition has become somewhat ambiguous, and several experts have strived to define it. The specialized debate started in the 1970s, as the names of orchestration authors started appearing on movie soundtracks or credits. Without meaning to generalize, European and foreign composers usually write the whole of their music, while in the States – and in the Hollywood industry especially – composition and instrumentation are considered two very different phases. This approach, however, is not univocal: composers, as any other kind of artist, do not all possess the same talent and expertise. Experience creates style as well as a working ground – especially when a specific movie genre is concerned – in which the composer becomes a conceptual and technical expert. As we shall see from different statements – both complimentary and critical – the writing method for functional music in Hollywood scores is fairly standardized. With a few rare exceptions, hardly any composer in Hollywood is "complete" in the most obvious sense established by Western musical tradition.

Since the dawn of the *talkies* in the 1930s, as American production studios started to require music for their first talking movies (especially the most spectacular ones such as adventures and dramas), it has been customary for them to hire a composer to write the music and provide the orchestrating staff with the score's main themes or, at best, its full piano sheet. In reality, the composer often supplies a simple melodic line, especially if the piece is merely one of the movie's many secondary moments. Every composer has aides who know his style, his timbric choices, and other features of his orchestral sound. Since each score lasts about one - one and a half hour (for dynamic movie genres such as action, thriller, adventure) writing, adjusting, re-writing, re-cording and adapting a score is burdensome work, and a single person could never accomplish it in such a short time. Therefore, though this is rarely acknowledged, orchestrators usually participate in the actual composing process. In this sense they are ghostwriters, similar to those working on movie scripts or, in the literary world, on books authored by better-known (but less-prepared) writers. They work like an editor may sometimes do when re-writing and improving, from a stylistic point of view at least, a book he is preparing for publication. This kind of activity is usually not credited, especially in the literary world, where authorship is considered essential to preserve a book's intellectual integrity. In movie scores, the "paternity" of each piece (especially secondary ones) tends to be overlooked. The open acknowledgement of orchestrators on the cover notes of published records especially in more recent times, is probably due to the growing demands of unions, becoming stronger each year. Although this may not always be the case, orchestrators are usually composers in their own right, with a solid professional background, who consider movies as a training ground for a future job in composition, or see it as an almost artisanal choice. Some orchestrators work exclusively with one composer, almost for the course of their entire career, always maintaining a low profile and contributing not only to the assimilation, but to the actual creation of the composer's style; Goldsmith's main aides, Arthur Morton and Alexander Courage, are two emblematic examples.

The open acknowledgement of orchestrators is a fairly recent acquisition, although ever since the so-called Golden Age – going from 1930s to the early 1960s – every major composer (Korngold, Waxman, Steiner, Tiomkin) has had an aide. The only difference with the following period is the fact that, at the time, orchestrators worked behind the scenes; only in later years would their contribution be acknowledged, and justice be done to their work. Orchestration, however, remains an unobtrusive phase, best appreciated by insiders. Concert-music composers, accustomed to a different kind of work, cannot fully comprehend the mentality and methods of movie scoring. For this and other reasons, first-rate composers such as Igor Stravinsky (1882-1971) and Maurice Ravel (1875-1937) often had rather negative experiences in movie scoring. Mario Castelnuovo-Tedesco – whom we already mentioned as one of Goldsmith's teachers – was an accomplished composer who worked for a long time in American movies and was always given free rein with his timbric choices. However, he mostly and consistently operated as a ghostwriter, in the sense that he added music to scores that had already been written.

We shall now examine more closely how composers act towards their aides, keeping standard working procedures in mind. In some cases, the orchestrator merely follows the composer's directions, when the latter does not have time to work on a score firsthand. In other cases, very prolific composers are substantially (and unofficially) helped during the actual writing process. This practice is rarely officially acknowledged, although other musicians, accustomed to working firsthand on their whole composition, have often hinted at it: such is the case with Leonard Rosenman (1924-2008) who, during an interview,[34] said:

> There are many people [composers, a/n] who have 30 people writing music for them. They can't read or write music.

The interviewer then asked if he was referring to ghostwriters, to which Rosenman replied:

> Yes. They don't call themselves ghost writers, they call themselves orchestrators, because it's illegal in the union [of American Composers, a/n] to be a ghost writer.

Music scholar Prendergast also approached this theme, highlighting how most of the criticism towards standard working methods was due to the deceptive notion, both in Hollywood and elsewhere, that Bernard Herrmann was

---

[34] DANIEL MANGODT, *Interview with Leonard Rosenman*, part 2, in "Soundtrack! The collector's quarterly", vol.14, no.56, December 1994, p.4. Rosenman was also a concert composer: hence his critical stance, similar to Bernard Herrmann's, against third-party orchestrations.

The only major film composer in Hollywood who does his own orchestrations.[35]

This "myth" lived on in the first historical essays on American movie scoring, such as Tony Thomas' *Music for the Movies*.[36] Pendergast underlines the surviving reservations towards this working method, although, in the 1950s, critic and orchestrator Lawrence Morton, whose comments below were quoted by Pendergast, was already describing it as everything but an anomaly. Herrmann himself, after all, often reasserted that he felt like an exception in his own field, although he harshly criticized the prevailing methods. When examining the passing of the torch between composer and orchestrator, we might summarize by saying that the former (as Goldsmith often did) usually creates a piano score or a few pentagrams containing every feature of the actual composition. As Lawrence Morton says:

> The final judgment as to the correctness, style, and practicability of an orchestrator's work can only be made by the composer. Criticism may thereafter voice the opinion that it doesn't like the composition of the orchestration, but only the composer can say if it matches his conception of what he wants to hear. And it would seem to me that if the orchestration is proper to the music, it should make no difference who did it.[37]

Delving further into practical methods, Morton provides a few examples:

> Many composers' sketches are so complete as to make the orchestrator nothing more than a glorified copyist. One Hollywood orchestrator, when asked to describe his job, replied, 'I take the music off the white paper and put in on the yellow'. (...) In such instances the orchestrator's discretion may be exercised only in such matters as assigning a phrase to the third clarinet instead of the second, spelling off the trombones in a lengthy passage requiring frequent change of position, making a practical division of labor between two percussion players, or deciding whether the harp part would be better notated in flats or sharps.[38]

---

[35] Roy M. Prendergast, *op.cit.*, p.85.
[36] See chapter 1, note 16.
[37] Lawrence Morton, *quoted* in Prendergast, *op.cit.*, p.85-86.
[38] *Ibid.*, p.86.

Cultured composers working in movies are rare, but among them Aaron Copland (1900-1990) is an emblematic case:

> Aaron Copland, for example, always used orchestrators when he worked in Hollywood. The reason it is not evident in his music, according to Morton, is that his sketches are so complete 'that no other musical personality has an opportunity to intrude itself upon his music'.[39]

Prendergast concludes by asserting that:

> Other composers who have worked in Hollywood who also are known for their complete sketches include Adolph Deutsch, Hugo Friedhofer, David Raksin, Alex North, Leonard Rosenman, Jerry Goldsmith, to name only a few.[40]

Herrmann's supposed integrity, therefore, can be considered just another working method, rather than an exclusive guarantee of excellence. His musical value is often superior to many of his colleagues', but a composition should not be considered shoddy for the mere fact of being orchestrated by someone else; especially considering that the composer's indications may be perfectly clear from the *expanded piano score* sketch. Criticism towards composers that are less prepared to the use

---

[39] PRENDERGAST, *Film Music*, p.86. Copland, however, criticized the movie system as a whole, especially the cutting of music in the editing phase. His only Oscar, for William Wyler's *The Heiress* (1950) surprised him greatly, as he considered the film's final score to be very far from his early intentions. On Copland's movie scoring and his difficult, albeit frequent, relationship with this medium, a few books are worth consulting: AARON COPLAND and VIVIAN PERLIS, *Copland: 1900 through 1942*, New York, St.Martin's/Marek, 1984 and, by the same authors, *Copland since 1943*, St.Martin's Press, 1989. The two volumes examine the musical "loans" in the composer's body of work, also in relation to popular singing (the scores for *The Red Pony*, *The Heiress*, *The North Star* and *The Cummington Story* are also examined). About the function of music in *The Red Pony*, based on the Steinbeck novel (Goldsmith wrote the score for its 1973 remake), see also ROBERT E.MORSBERGER, *Of Mice and Music: Scoring Steinbeck Movies in Honor of Tetsumaro Hayashi*; Athens, Ohio University Press, 1994.

[40] PRENDERGAST, *ibid.*, p.86.

of orchestras may be more justified. This often happens, in movie scoring, when pop or rock musicians are hired for the sole fact of possessing an easy melodic ability. In this case, the orchestrator – not unlike the editor to some celebrity memoir – is essential for reaching the movie's aim. Even a successful composer like Erich Wolfgang Korngold, who, in his early years in Vienna, had written a few operas and a considerable quantity of orchestral music, was helped by orchestrators upon his arrival to Los Angeles – namely, future movie composer Hugo Friedhofer (1902-81) and Milan Roder (1878-1956); such an "industrial" conception of musical writing does not in any way lessen, in Hollywood mentality, the actual authorship of music. John Williams himself worked on his great orchestral scores, revisiting the spirit of Korngold's adventure scores, with the help of Herbert W. Spencer, substituting his usual aide John Neufeld.

Bernard Herrmann and Miklós Rózsa, classical composers in culture and rank, were much less prolific than their colleagues. Both highlighted their complete autonomy even (or especially) as far as rhythm (in Herrmann's case) or orchestral color (in Rózsa's case) were concerned. Thanks to their smaller production, they could give more attention to detail, though we will later see how each of them had a very different approach to instrumentation: uncompromising the former, more accommodating the latter.

According to Smith's account, Herrmann often crossed paths with Goldsmith when they both worked at Universal. Here is another snippet of their tumultuous relationship:

> As Goldsmith's star in Hollywood rose, Herrmann's bitterness grew in proportion. One afternoon in 1962 as he walked to the Universal lot, Goldsmith – then scoring his first major film, *Lonely Are the Brave* – heard the screeching voice of his ex-mentor from across the street: 'You're like all the other Hollywood guys, using an orchestrator!' [41]

---

[41] STEVEN C. SMITH, *A Heart at Fire's Center*, op.cit., p. 205.

Throughout his career Herrmann stated, in no uncertain terms, what he considered to be a composer's moral integrity, an opinion later confirmed by Ennio Morricone: never allowing anyone else to intervene in the practice of composition. Rózsa, despite his reservations, was forced to adapt in order to meet his deadlines, though he always defended his autonomy of choice, even when orchestration was concerned. As he himself said:

> When I did my second picture, Lady Hamilton,[42] the union said I would not be allowed to orchestrate. I had to look for an orchestrator, something I had never done in my life. I was accustomed to writing the score, first in very loose sketches, then in full score. Now I had to start out writing exact sketches. The Italians call this process *spartita* (sic) – condensed score. You can learn it, and I did. I tried many orchestrators, and my scores sounded as if they had been written by someone else. I told the orchestrators, 'Don't write in anything I haven't written down', but they said, 'We will make it sound lush.' I said, 'Don't make it lush, leave it as it is.' I finally found a man who did what I wanted with the score. With the Hollywood tempo, it is not possible to write out the full score.[43]

From the Hungarian composer's words we can understand how, even since the first scores for talkies, the unions defending musicians' rights were quite vigilant. The artistic freedom left to contributors is also apparent, given the fact that Rózsa himself felt compelled to enforce some limitations to their musical additions. Rózsa also reminds us that the work of contributors, whether they be called "*orchestrators*", "*secondary composers*" or, more ambiguously, "*ghostwriters*", remains essential when considering the extremely tight deadlines for the creation of a cinematic score. Truth be told, after a period of intense work during the '40s (especially in *noir* movies), the Hungarian composer had much more time at his disposal when working on the great histor-

---

[42] *Lady Hamilton*, also known as *That Hamilton Woman*: directed by Alexander Korda, (1941) and starring Vivien Leigh and Sir Laurence Olivier.

[43] Rózsa's comment as reported by RUSSELL LACK, *Twenty Four Frames Under – A Buried History of Film Music*, London, Quartet Books, 1997, p.189.

ical-religious scores he created for MGM (meaning, of course, that deadlines were more generous than usual, though they rarely extended over more than a year).

Among younger composers, the practice of leaving orchestration to contributors has become widespread, with two or more names often showing up on credits. An extreme example is given by Michael Kamen's music for *Robin Hood: Prince of Thieves* (1991; directed by Kevin Reynolds), for which no less than sixteen orchestrators were credited, including Kamen himself as well as composers Don Davis and Chris Boardman. The request for music, considered necessary to underline images, grew exponentially with the popularity of adventure and action movies, as a symptom of an ever-accelerating productive demand. Goldsmith himself, in quick statements following his European concerts, was known to criticize the working methods of younger composers. In May 2000, after playing at London's Barbican Centre with the London Symphony Orchestra, the American composer criticized such scores as those for *Gladiator* (2000; directed by Ridley Scott; music by Hans Zimmer, with additional contribution by Lisa Gerrard). In this case, as in many other from the Hollywood industry in the mid-'90s, he believed composers to be "at the mercy" of orchestrators. As for his own work, in contrast, he stated:

> [My] own sketches are so complete that the orchestrator is doing little more than a copyist.[44]

Goldsmith's judgment regarding the composers' excessive subordination to orchestrators is in tune with the criticism expressed (especially in Europe) towards the American movie-scoring method, disrespectful of the "sacred" aspects of composition. Goldsmith's example, the score for *Gladiator*, is rather emblematic, as is almost any score from composer Hans Zimmer's "factory". The latter especially, since the mid-90s, often promoted young musicians contributing to his projects, be it as

---

[44]   This and the previous statements are found in "Soundtrack! The collector's quarterly", vol.19, no.74, Summer 2000, p.20.

composers, additional composers, orchestrators or arrangers. In *Gladiator*'s case there were two official composers (Zimmer and Gerrard), one additional composer (Klaus Badelt, who later started working on his own), plus six orchestrators; Gavin Greenaway, who had already worked with Zimmer as an additional composer, was the score's conductor. A veritable example of teamwork, renouncing strict authorship in favor of an undoubtedly quicker execution, and providing the finished product – usually an action movie – with a functional and exponentially growing musical backdrop.

European composers like Morricone, on the other hand, remind us that arrangers[45] usually worked in the shadows. Controversy arose, in fact, when the Italian maestro himself was forced to work as a ghostwriter. In some rare instances, younger American composers are appreciated by their European colleagues both for their musical solutions and for writing *all* of their music. In this respect, it is significant to notice Italian composer Franco Piersanti's statement during his talk with Sergio Miceli:

> Howard Shore... Carter Burwell... they seem to me more like European than American musicians. (...) Two [North] American composers among the few to make their own orchestrations. And, if they ever had some help in composing, I believe they did it for a question of schedule rather than ability.[46]

Canadian Howard Shore and American Carter Burwell, respectively chosen by such directors as David Cronenberg and Joel and Ethan Coen, are odd men out in a system envisioning an almost uncompromising division of work, even in the case of a creative process such as musical composition.[47] Although neither Shore nor Burwell had a solid

---

[45]   Arranger and Orchestrator are not synonyms, but Morricone's statement applies to a time, at the beginning of his career, when it was customary to distribute melodies to instruments as quickly as possible.

[46]   SERGIO MICELI, *Musica e cinema nella cultura del novecento*, Florence, Sansoni, 2000, pp.507-508.

[47]   It's worth noticing, however, that Shore himself was often helped by orchestrators like Homer Denison. Shore later became famous for writing, orchestrating and conducting

concert career background, their work was nonetheless more sophist-icated and polished: they, too, felt the need to proactively intervene in all phases, conduction included, of movie scoring – though conducting does not make them in any way exceptional; see the example of Woj-ciech Kilar, a Polish composer who, though he did not conduct, wrote all of his music both for movies and for concerts. What further aston-ishes European composers and musicologists is the fact that, in many cases, composers had worked as orchestrators for others in their youth – Goldsmith himself, during the 1950s, arranged and orchestrated mu-sic for second-rate Hollywood composers such as Lionel Newman and Joseph Gershenson. The aforementioned Don Davis, who wrote the score for *The Matrix* (1999; directed by the Wachowski siblings), as well as others like Mark McKenzie and William Ross, went from a support-ing to a leading composing role, often (ironically) leaving orchestra-tions to others.

Ennio Morricone, on the other hand, often reiterated his conviction that orchestration, being a basic part of composition, could not be done by others, not even the closest of aides. His opinions on the matter are as uncompromising as Bernard Herrmann's.[48] In his monography on Morricone, and based on the maestro's opinions, Miceli judges the so-called "arrangements" of movie scores to which the maestro himself worked both before and after the start of his actual career in movies (in 1961), as:

> Typically clandestine work, very common at the time, to which Morricone complied roughly from 1958 to 1969, and of which I believe useless to provide a detailed account.[49]

Further on, Miceli briefly describes Morricone's work in this realm,

---

the score for Peter Jackson's trilogy based on *The Lord of the Rings* (2001-2003), for which he was awarded three Oscars among the total of 17 won by the trilogy.

[48] Miceli, *Musica e cinema...*, op.cit., pg.487-88. The chat with Morricone was reported in the first edition of this study, as well: Sergio Miceli, *La musica nel film- Arte e artigianato*, Fiesole, Discanto, 1982, p.327-328.

[49] Miceli, *Morricone, la musica, il cinema*, op.cit., p.88.

stating the composer's extreme difficulty in dealing with such confused situations in terms of rights and authorship. It is underlined, however, that working on somebody else's music – be it for adaptation, arrangement, or any kind of contribution dictated by pragmatism and experience – is a thankless and unrewarding chore, which Morricone himself could hardly bear to remember. Starting from this "undergrowth", which at the time was not just limited to the musical aspect of Italian movies, it is understandable that critics should base their judgment of American movies on the same strict parameters. But the situation in the U.S. is actually quite different, chiefly because musicians working on the final version of a score are always acknowledged and credited. Their contribution is shown and their names are known – what is more, for the most part, orchestrators also have their own aides. If any doubt remains, it concerns the actual "weight" of their contribution to a composition. Morricone is perfectly right in stating that music belongs to those who conceive it, from the first sketch to the last phrasing: such a statement on his part is justified, and almost predictable. But when examining the most experienced American composers, should we exclusively base our opinion on official movie credits, it is nonetheless at the very least difficult to judge Goldsmith and Williams, as well as their younger colleagues like Elliot Goldenthal, Basil Poledouris, James Horner, Christopher Young etc., as incapable of orchestrating.[50] One look at the movie work of "classic" composers, such as Erich Korngold and Franz Waxman, is enough to understand that it all boils down to a question of deadlines. Korngold, as we previously said, had been very successful before coming to Hollywood – first as an *enfant prodige* and later as a "fulfilled promise" –, but he simply accepted the U.S. system, working with aides who knew his music and helped him write his scores; the same can be said of Waxman, who had composed cantatas like *Das Lied von Terezin*, as well as a remarkable violin

---

[50]   Among the aforementioned composers, Goldenthal was very active in theatre; Horner, on the other hand, since reaching artistic maturity during the mid-90s always wrote all of his music, including orchestrations: he scored such movies as *Apollo 13* (1995), *Braveheart* (1995) and *Titanic* (1997).

and orchestra piece, from 1946, based on themes from Bizet's *Carmen* and which was added to the repertoire of violin virtuoso Jascha Heifetz.

For the most part, therefore, orchestrators were employed so that "official" composers would not be distracted from their composing task, though they still had the duty to supervise the final result. From a strictly technical point of view, the degree of orchestral and dynamic complexity found in Goldsmith's and Williams' scores is often astounding; the same can be said, in a more "traditional" sense, for the generation including Korngold, Steiner and Newman, as well as their younger colleagues. Behind any musical composition there must be a controlling figure ensuring the structural wholeness of such a complex piece of work. In the most extreme cases, composers are at the helm of "composing teams" and, among other things, they almost invariably have the task of conducting their music. From this fact only we might conclude that the use of aides is due – as well as to working unions, as we previously said – to the excessive workload that any major movie composer is expected to accomplish in the course of a few weeks or, at best, a few months.[51]

An ambiguous counter-example occurs when orchestration becomes a fundamental part of a composer's style. Such was the case with Thomas Pasatieri, who, after writing a few theatrical operas during the 1970s, in 1984 started to orchestrate for Hollywood composers like James Horner, and especially Thomas Newman. With the latter, Pasatieri forged a professional partnership spanning about 20 movies; since Newman's style[52] was more connected to timbre and rhythm rather

---

[51]   In the past there were exceptions: one of them was Rózsa, who was able to read up at length before composing big-budget scores such as *Ben-Hur* (1959) and *El Cid* (1961); for the latter, in particular, the Hungarian musician worked closely with scholars of ancient music in Spain, and he sojourned in Europe in order to study for the composition of a score that was supposed to be as "authentic" as possible; the shooting schedule for any historical-religious movie, at the time, was much more ample, allowing time for every component to be examined in depth.

[52]   Thomas Newman was the son of the aforementioned Alfred Newman, one of the fathers of movie scoring in Hollywood and longtime head of 20th Century-Fox's music department.

than to melody, we might say that almost half the work pertained to his orchestrator; the use of percussions in *American Beauty* (1999; directed by Sam Mendes) or *Erin Brockovich* (2000; directed by Steven Soderbergh) are two pertinent examples. Whenever melody, rhythm and harmony are dominant, authorship cannot be questioned: but the work of Newman and Pasatieri does raise some questions. Newman and Pasatieri's long and symbiotic collaboration echoes Jerry Goldsmith's relationship with Arthur Morton; these professional associations, somehow, resulted in a peculiar orchestrating style that makes it hard to discern the composer's work from the orchestrator's. Another, more recent example (just as free from negative connotations as the one of Newman and Pasatieri) is the work of NY composer Elliot Goldenthal (a pupil of John Corigliano's) with his longtime orchestrator Robert Elhai. In this case, the orchestrator's duty is essentially to support Goldenthal, fully conscious of the fact that the composer's style and timbric choices verge towards poly-stylism, closer to avant-gardes than to Romantic melodic tradition: some examples of this composite style are the scores for *Heat* (1995; directed by Michael Mann), two Batman movies (*Batman Forever*, 1995; *Batman and Robin*, 1997; both directed by Joel Schumacher), *Titus* (2000; directed by Julie Taymor), and *Final Fantasy - The Spirits Within* (2001; directed by Hironobu Sakaguchi). Goldenthal's movie work has made him famous, though he currently devotes himself to the composition of concerts commissioned by musical institutions (among them a funeral oratory, a personal interpretation of a mass, and a ballet inspired by Shakespeare's *Othello*).

European musicians, as we said, hardly ever work this way: their difference in method has led to a smaller number of scores for each composer (with notable, more prolific exceptions such as Morricone, French composer Philippe Sarde and others);[53] this, in theory, should result in more polished works, though usually with a reduced orchestral component, so as to be managed even by composers with average abilities in orchestration. Remarkably, when compared to the European film in-

---

[53] Philippe Sarde, a musical contributor for directors like Claude Sautet, Bertrand Tavernier and Marco Ferreri, usually requires aides for orchestration, as well as for conducting.

dustry, the volume of U.S. movie productions appears enormous; the need to provide almost every movie with a score that is functional to its scenes – while maintaining a high technical and orchestral level – means that only a handful of composers are capable of producing (in a literal sense) up to four or five scores a year; such is the case with the most in-demand composers, meaning those who are able to offer the best results. This is why, in a production scheme ruled by "assembly lines", music is subjected to the exact same parameters of any other aspect.

After Korngold and Steiner's emigration and subsequent high-pro-file roles in American movie scoring, a similar experience occurred to an Italian composer, the aforementioned Mario Castelnuovo-Tedesco. This talented musician left Italy for the U.S. in July 1939, and in 1940 he was still facing great hardship in his new country; by the end of the same year, financial reasons forced him to start working for Met-ro-Goldwyn-Mayer. From that moment on he started a frequent co-operation with the movie world, first as an MGM employee and later as a freelance composer. His contribution was rarely officially acknow-ledged. In most cases, he worked almost clandestinely, adding musical pieces to pre-existing scores: not exactly rewarding work for a com-poser who had already been successful in Italy, and had been forced to flee his country by Fascist racial laws. In his *Memorie*,[54] the Florentine composer recalled his disappointing work for MGM. This is how Malor-gio summarizes it:

> The composer found himself victim of a world where music was con-sidered a "screw in a well-oiled machine", that is to say, a mere "filler". Castelnuovo-Tedesco was not allowed to participate in the movie's cre-ation, but was forced to write music according to producers' taste. Worst of all, he had to share the scoring process with other composers, leaving his pieces to be orchestrated by arrangers. This fact particularly bothered him, as the Tuscan musician was notoriously capable of writing a whole opera complete with its *libretto*. Although, after one year at MGM, the mu-

---

[54] More precisely in chapter 77, entitled 'Hollywood': this passage is summarized in Cosimo Malorgio, *Censure di un musicista- La vicenda artistica e umana di Mario Castelnuovo-Tedesco*, Milan, Paravia, 2001, p.26.

sic department director acknowledged his talent and allowed him to orchestrate a score for the first time, he jokingly kept referring to his work there as "the years of slavery in Babylon".[55]

As opposed to other 20th century musicians who managed to be prolific in concert music, while at the same time working successfully for the silver screen, – such as British composers William Walton (1902-83) and Ralph Vaughan-Williams (1872-1958) – Castelnuovo Tedesco's contributions were an end in themselves and did not make their mark on American movies. Of course the studios had the last word in choosing the music they required, but no talented musician had ever lacked the chance to give his personal and original contribution, without ever needing to challenge the industry. Later on, Castelnuovo-Tedesco started working as a teacher: among his pupils were many up-and-coming Hollywood composers of the time, including Henry Mancini, André Previn and Jerry Goldsmith. As highlighted by James Westby,[56] Castelnuovo-Tedesco played four different roles in movie scoring, spanning the 250-some projects he contributed to: as a supporting or co-author (in most movies, especially during his time at MGM), as the composer of a whole score (e.g. René Clair's And Then There Were None, 1945); as a source music composer (operatic pieces, ballets); and, finally, as the writer of a movie score that was later used for another project.[57] Once more, it is apparent that he mostly worked as a ghostwriter, which is generally considered an entirely different job from being an orchestrator. Rosenman, as we reported earlier, regards this activity as illegal, though it is not unusual for a composer to work on a score started or even completed by somebody else. Sometimes, the additional music is so significant that the "supporting" composer is almost as important as the "official" one: a poignant example is the prologue written by Gold-

---

[55] Ibid, p.26.
[56] James Westby, 'Mario Castelnuovo-Tedesco', in New Grove (2nd ed.), vol.5, p.255-258.
[57] The practice of "recycling" existing movie scores is still in use and involves many composers; the best-known examples are the scores by John Williams, Jerry Goldsmith and James Horner, often reused on sequels scored by different composers.

smith for *The Agony and the Ecstasy* (1965; directed by Carol Reed). The score had been written by Alex North but the composer, due to previous engagements, was unable to work on the prologue, which had been added later and was supposed to consist in a twelve minute-long symphonic poem about Michelangelo. A more recent example is the cooperation between Trevor Jones and Randy Edelman on *The Last of the Mohicans* (1992; directed by Michael Mann) and between Goldsmith and Joel McNeely on *Air Force One* (1997; directed by Wolfgang Petersen); in both cases, Jones and Goldsmith wrote the score, while Edelman and McNeely were later hired to complete some sequences or replace some of the weaker passages. We previously saw how composing a score, even for less sophisticated movies, is no simple task. Composers, in these cases, become little more than pawns; even an artist as experienced as Goldsmith could see his score being rejected, replaced or cut to make room for new music, often written by others. We cited a few examples where musical "authorship" is obvious: but in most cases, as with Castelnuovo-Tedesco's work, secondary passages are often left to ghostwriters, who might even be orchestrators entrusted with completing a composer's score. Even Goldsmith was sometimes forced to accept the help of aides in the most delicate phases of composition, providing orchestrators with a full sketch and the indications on how to write the score. The actual work of a composer like Goldsmith can be better understood by comparing his method to the one Sergej Prokof'ev had devised, for practical reasons, when writing his concert works. The latter is described by Prendergast, who quotes Victor Seroff, as follows:

> This practice of orchestrating from highly detailed sketches [is not] restricted to the film-music world. Prokofiev, with the iron exception of his score to the film Alexander Nevsky, had all of his scores orchestrated from detailed sketches. As Victor Seroff points out, 'Prokofiev devised a system that permitted him not to lose time on the long trips across the country. Because the vibration of the train made it impossible to write the orchestral score, he did all the preparatory work by marking in his piano score which of the instruments was to play this or that melody or passage, in-

cluding the indications for accents and dynamics, so that when he left the train and found himself for a short time on 'firm ground' all he had to do was to copy automatically his indications into the orchestral score. At first it seemed impossible to write into the piano score the names of the instruments, particularly when the chords occupied all the staffs, but with practice he succeeded. He was pleased with having perfected this method, for it allowed him to turn over the piano score to a capable musician who could the easily transcribe it into the orchestral score'.[58]

Undoubtedly, when a composer, was also a valid conductor like Goldsmith, it is hard to believe that the whole instrumental phase could be handled by others; it is a fact, however, that very few movie and record credits mention him as an orchestrator, with the exception of *Studs Lonigan* (1962), *The Stripper* (1963), *Babe* (1975), *The Cassandra Crossing* (1976), *The Edge* (1997) and *Hollow Man* (2000). We might, however, intuitively believe his working method to be similar to Prokof'ev's and assume that his orchestrators only made secondary choices. After the start of his career, for a few decades Goldsmith was helped by Arthur Morton (1908-2000), with whom he kept close contact until he died.[59] Despite being a composer in his own right, Morton devoted himself to the music of his younger associate and colleague for more than thirty years; being the more experienced of the two – he had worked in TV and movies for more than two decades – Morton inevitably influenced and enriched Goldsmith's "workshop" with advice and possibly (though the latter is just an hypothesis) something more. Their symbiotic relationship was similar, with due distinctions, to the one between jazz musicians Duke Ellington and Billy Strayhorn. Sometime later, Goldsmith started working with Alexander Courage[60] (1919-2008), who

[58]   PRENDERGAST, *Film Music*, op.cit., p.85.

[59]   Arthur Morton wrote scores for TV shows, but, since the 1940s, mostly worked as an orchestrator and an arranger. His professional relationship with Goldsmith started in the mid-60s and ended in 1997 with the score for *L.A.Confidential*.

[60]   Alexander Courage had an active role as a composer, working almost exclusively for television, though his main role was as orchestrator and conductor. He worked sporadically with John Williams as well as with Goldsmith and, less recently, with Jerome Moross, participating in quite a few musical adaptations for the silver screen.

was also a composer and the author of the famous *Star Trek* TV series main theme (originally on air from 1966 to 1969); Goldsmith later scored several of the show's big-screen versions.[61] Courage's work with Goldsmith was less assiduous than Morton's – the two colleagues often worked on the same movie, especially during the '80s and '90s – though he still became Goldsmith's tireless *alter ego*. Courage retired in 2000, and Goldsmith's last projects were supported by a younger composer named Mark McKenzie.[62] During the early years of Goldsmith's career, on the other hand, David Tamkin (1906-75)[63] had been his main helper, especially when working on Western movie scores. Without wishing to make a strict stylistic distinction between the composer's two main orchestrators, it is apparent that Morton was chosen as an aide for the most complex scores, which we may even define experimental in timbre and sound effects, as well as in musical language; Courage's projects were usually adventure movies or thrillers where Goldsmith's recognizable and syncopated style merged well with the orchestra's virtuosism and with an instrumentation closer to the style of Strauss and Respighi, especially remarkable for its use of brass, woods and percussions.

For about a quarter of a century, Morton worked on more than a hundred scores – that is without counting his work on TV series – tackling all of Goldsmith's cinematic genres: western (*Rio Conchos, Bandolero!*), adventure (*Papillon, The Wind and the Lion, Lionheart*), science fiction (*Planet of the Apes, Logan's Run, Capricorn One, Alien, Star Trek I, Outland, Star Trek V*), horror (*The Omen, Damien - Omen II, The Final Conflict, The Mephisto Waltz, The Other*), thriller (*The Boys from Brazil, Warlock, The River Wild*), action (*The Last Run, Total Recall*), war (*Patton, MacArthur, Inchon*), comedy (*Dennis the Menace, I.Q.*), drama (*Islands in the*

---

[61] Goldsmith contributed to chapters one (1979), five (1989), eight (1996), nine (1998) and ten (2002) of the science fiction saga.

[62] He wrote by himself the scores for a few lesser-known movies, the most remarkable being *The Disappearance of Garcia Lorca* (1997, directed by Marcos Zurinaga).

[63] Tamkin was an authentic ghostwriter who, from the late '30 to the late '60, produced a significant number of orchestrations – for Westerns especially – as well as additional music for several second-rate movies.

Stream, Angie), noir (*Chinatown, L.A.Confidential*). This selection of titles, including all of Goldsmith's most famous movies and, in some cases, the most successful of his career, is proof that Morton had somehow become the composer's *doppelganger*. Morton's retirement brought an end to Goldsmith's most "experimental" period in orchestration, perfectly exemplified by the unusual us of wind instruments in the *Planet of the Apes* score. The latter included an absence of mouthpieces on French horns, clarinets whose keys were pressed without a note, a wider percussive section where the customary piano and xylophone were used in tandem with more unusual instruments: *cuika* (a Brazilian drum with a stick in the center, producing impressive monkey-like sounds), *vibraslap* (a small instrument made out of two pieces of wood clashing together), kitchen mixing bowls (empty half-spheres of steel),[64] and more. Goldsmith's work with Morton continued during the '70s with a more traditional approach to instrumentation. Among the best scores of this decade, *Papillon* (1973), *Islands in the Stream* (1977), *The Boys from Brazil* (1978) and *Capricorn One* (1978) show a few remarkable peculiarities, such as the use of solo French horn in *Islands in the Stream* and of percussions in *Capricorn One*. The latter's MAIN TITLE is also worth noticing, as it became a model of sorts for other Goldsmith overtures such as the one for *Night Crossing* (1981; directed by Delbert Mann) and, later, the one for *Total Recall* (1990), which can be defined as a syncopated (or "limping") march.

1979 was an important year for the two musicians, as they found themselves working on two science fiction productions for 20th Century-Fox and Paramount: *Alien* (directed by Ridley Scott) and *Star Trek. The Motion Picture* (directed by Robert Wise), respectively. While the first was a piece of musical and cinematic bravura, the second, due to its quick preparation and shooting,[65] was rather lacking in dramatic power. Its score, however, showed a remarkable search for unusual sound effects and combinations, such as the use of the Blaster Beam.

---

[64] Goldsmith took it upon himself to bring everyday objects to be employed for unusual sounds.

[65] The script, when shooting started, was also incomplete.

Goldsmith's aide brought him closer to electronic music, which the composer used sparingly. Synthesizers and other artificial sound machines were only fundamental in a few scores with less-than-memorable results, such as the ones for *Runaway* (1984; directed by Michael Crichton), *Criminal Law* (1988; directed by Martin Campbell) and *Link* (1986; directed by Richard Franklin). With the exception of instruments like the *Echoplex* – used in *Patton* to produce the echoing sound of two trumpets, suggesting a great distance – it was only in the 1980s that the composer, with trusty Morton by his side, started integrating orchestra and electronics in a sparing and complimentary manner. In *Gremlins* (1984; directed by Joe Dante) this use is more extensive, though aesthetically justified:

> The electronics in *Gremlins*, which are the 'voice' of [the] creatures, mix well with the standard orchestra, and in a sense work as a counterpoint to the 'serious' traditional instruments.[66]

The composer confirms this commentator's statement, briefly recounting his experience:

> I wanted sort of an animalistic sound to [the creatures]. It's comical, and musical. Joe Dante's a fun person to work with. He enjoys music, and he wants a lot of music in his films. It turned out the crazier I got, the more he liked it. When I played for him the 'Gremlin Rag', this funky way-out tune, he practically fell on the floor. Because it was just what he wanted, something totally out of left field.[67]

Later on, electronic integration would become an almost constant feature in Goldsmith and Morton's orchestrations. A remarkable example was the score for *Total Recall* (1990; directed by Verhoeven), where artificial sounds were meant to play an impressionistic and complimentary role (see the introduction to the track THE HOLOGRAM); percussions, on the other hand, were fundamental in providing the irregular pulsation

---

[66] DAVID MORGAN, *Knowing the Score*, New York, Harper Collins, 2000, p.178.
[67] *Ibid.*, p.178-179.

which would later become so crucial to Goldsmith's rhythm.

More examples of Goldsmith and Morton's orchestra technique are: *King Solomon's Mines* (1985; directed by Jack Lee Thompson), showing a significant and possibly excessive presence of march brass, and a virtuoso use of diffused percussions such as the xylophone; *Medicine Man* (1991; directed by John McTiernan), with light, Caribbean-like percussions inspired by the Brazilian landscape; the use of tuba and harmonica as solo instruments for comedic purposes in *Dennis the Menace* (1993; directed by Nick Castle); *City Hall* (1995; directed by Harold Becker), an urban thriller showing an extensive use of percussions, similar to the technique employed by Leonard Bernstein on his 1954 cinematic masterpiece *On the Waterfront* (directed by Elia Kazan).

Instrumentation in Alien

For this science-fiction movie, Goldsmith created a musical language rich in non-traditional techniques; he and Morton worked extensively with strings, though the most remarkable part of this score is how it mixes a symphonic orchestra with unusual tribal or folkloric instruments: the traditional aboriginal *didjeridoo*, the middle-eastern, oboe-like *shawm*, the old-fashioned *serpent*; the *conch* or *shell trumpet*, a wind instrument built from a seashell. What follows is a brief description of these four instruments, all of which conferred a peculiar touch to the composer's frightening sounds from outer space.

Didjeridoo. A primitive ceremonial musical instrument hailing from northern Australia. It is an aboriginal wind instrument producing a hypnotic sound. Built from a green eucalyptus trunk, naturally made hollow by termites eating the organic substances inside its pith, it has an embouchure shaped with virgin beeswax to fit the player's lips. A standard version of this instrument is 70 to 180 centimeters long, but some can reach up to 250 centimeters. From a musical point of view it can be ascribed to the aerophone category. Its timbre changes according to the player's mouth through a "creative" use of tongue, voice and air pressure.[68]

---

[68]   PAPI MORENO, *Didjeridu- lo strumento a fiato degli aborigeni australiani*, Turin, Clerico Edi-

[example of Didjeridoo]

Shaum. In the *Alien* score, this woodwind can be found in the track FACE HUGGER IN THE LAB – a scene where the creature is analyzed after sticking to the space helmet of astronaut Kane – as well as in THE DROID, which was mostly deleted during the final editing phase. A double-reed instrument anticipating the oboe, the European *Shaum* was imported in the 13th century from open-air and military Arabian music. It is also traditionally found in Southern Italy (in the Calabria region, in particular, it is called a *pipita*). Its name shares a common root with French word *chalumeau*.[69]

tore, 2000, p.10-12.

[69] JAMES A.MACGILLIVRAY, *The Woodwind*, in ANTHONY BAINES (ed.), *Musical Instruments Through the Ages*, London, Penguin, 1961.

Serpent. Dating back to the 16th century, the instrument most probably hailed from France, as a double-bass to the *cornetto* family. Almost two and a half meters long, it is formed by a wide chestnut tube lined in black leather, with a curved shape like a snake's to allow the player's fingers to reach its six holes. The upper part has a deep ivory or horn mouthpiece. In large military bands from the last quarter of the 18th century, the Serpent was used as a grave support; and it was not until 1835, when the bass tuba and its relatives were introduced, that it was abandoned. It was used in various symphonic orchestras, like in Rossini's *Le siège de Corinthe* (1826), Mendelssohn's *Paulus* oratory (1836), Wagner's *Rienzi* (1842) and, later on, in Verdi's *Les Vêspres Siciliennes* (1855). Hector Berlioz mentions it in his essay on orchestration:

> The truly barbaric tone of this instrument would be much better suited for the bloody cult of the Druids than for that of the Catholic church, where it is still in use – as a monstrous symbol for the lack of understanding and the coarseness of taste and feeling which have governed the application of music in our churches since times immemorial. Only one case is to be excepted: masses for the dead, where the serpent serves to double the dreadful choir of the Dies Irae. Here its cold and awful blaring is doubtless of mournful poetry when accompanying this text, imbued with all the horrors of death and the revenge of an irate God. The instrument might also be used in secular compositions based on similar ideas; but its use must be limited to this purpose only. Moreover, its tone blends poorly with the other timbres of the orchestra and of voices. As the bass of a great mass of wind instruments it cannot match the bass tuba or even the ophicleide.[70]

The French composer used it in the *Agnus Dei* of his *Messe Solennelle* (1824), as a support to the second bassoon, although he later chose to employ the timbre of other bass instruments, such as trombones or even ophicleides (which he used during the presentation of *Dies Irae*, in the fifth movement of his *Symphonie Fantastique*). After the virtuoso period of the 16th century, this instrument was relegated to accompa-

---

[70] HECTOR BERLIOZ, *Grande traité d'instrumentation et d'orchestration modernes*. The quote is taken from the book's English translation, New York, Dover Publications, p.348.

nying Gregorian music in Catholic churches, which it did until the second half of the 19th century.[71] For *Alien*'s opening credits, as per the director's request, Goldsmith substituted his original piece (mostly conventional, though it showcased a remarkable trumpet solo) with a much more avant-garde version. This marked the first appearance of the serpent, twice and in two bars each time; in the following pieces, however, its timbre – together with the didjeridoo's – was employed to create the alien's grunting. On the *Alien* score LP[72] the serpent is distinctly audible in the track Breakaway (track#3) namely on the section starting at 1'21" from the beginning. In other tracks, such as Face Hugger (track#2) and The Droid (track#6), the serpent showcases its colder timbre. The serpent's presence is also constant In The Shaft (track#9), a track that was cut during the final editing process. Had it been included in the movie's final score, this piece would have proved a very interesting addition, as the serpent in it denoted the alien's visual (though not physical) absence. Its elimination reduced the score's dramatic result as Goldsmith has conceived it.

Conch (or *Shell trumpet*). A wind instrument made out of an empty seashell, specifically altered to produce a sound. Originally created for signaling, it is employed for ceremonial purposes as well, in the Fiji islands and elsewhere. This instrument usually emits a single note; harmonics are possible, though rarely used. The sound of the "seashell trumpet" is deep in every sense, as if coming from a faraway time and place. John Cage also employed this instrument in *Inlets* (1977).[73] In *Alien*, Goldsmith used it at the start of his avant-garde piece for the new opening credits, where on two separate occasions it played a figuration of four distinct notes (b.4-5 e b.11-12 of the handwritten sketch); all of them are F#, since most of these instruments can only produce a single note.

---

[71] Curt Sachs, *The History of Musical Instruments*, New York, W.W.Norton & Company, 1940, p.421.
[72] Silva Screen FilmCD003.
[73] Mitchell Clark, *Some basic on shell trumpets and some very basics on how to make them*, 1996: http://www.furious.com/perfect/shells.html.

[*Alien* (1979), *The Shaft*, 'Tailing theme']

Alexander Courage started working as an orchestrator after a TV composing career without praise or blame. In his youth he had learned his trade by working for the small screen and in lesser movie productions – westerns especially – though he glamorized his career by participating in the first few episodes of the *Star Trek* TV series, in the second half of the '60s. He worked with Goldsmith on about forty occasions. Their collaboration started on war movie *Morituri* (1965), and we might recall Courage conducting one of Goldsmith's westerns scores, the 1966 remake of *Stagecoach* (directed by Gordon Douglas).[74] During the '70s, Courage helped Goldsmith on two of his television works: *QB VII* (1974;

---

[74]   It is quite possible that, while working on this movie, Courage helped Goldsmith with orchestration, as well. This is implied in JEFF BOND, *The Music of Star Trek*, Lone Eagle, Los Angeles, 1999, p.14.

directed by Tom Gries) and *Babe* (1975; directed by Buzz Kulik). The first was somewhat influenced by Jewish music, and included an opening fanfare showcasing the composer's trademark irregular rhythm, and a remarkable use of choir. Goldsmith himself stated that the idea of giving a voice to the Jewish funeral prayer (*Kaddish*) would infuse the memory evoked by this ABC mini-series with a sense of authenticity. The collaboration between Goldsmith and Courage, however, only became consistent with *Legend* (1985; directed by Ridley Scott) and *Lionheart* (1987; directed by Franklin J. Schaffner). Later on they worked together on *First Knight* (1995), *The Ghost and the Darkness* (1996; directed by Stephen Hopkins), *Mulan* (1998; directed by Tony Bancroft and Barry Cook), *Small Soldiers* (1998; directed by Joe Dante) and the "twin scores" for *The Mummy* (1999; directed by Stephen Sommers) and *The 13th Warrior* (1999; directed by John McTiernan and Michael Crichton). Fairytale atmospheres and impressionistic instruments pervaded *Legend*, *Gremlins II- The New Batch* (1990)[75] and *Powder* (1996). Suggestive and complex were the scores for two of Paul Verhoeven's movies after *Total Recall*: *Basic Instinct* (1992) and *Hollow Man* (2000).

Basic Instinct's *Main theme*

While working together on *Basic Instinct*,[76] composer and orchestrator created a sensual and refined score, which was later defined a "study in passion devoid of feeling"[77] A wide but subtle use of electronics (Crossed Legs) joined by unbridled percussions and a frequent switch in melody among high-texture strings, brass and woodwind instruments (Night Life), framed by one of Goldsmith's most defining main themes, particularly remarkable for its instrumental distribution. The piece's structure is very simple: an exposition of the main theme, a

---

[75] In this movie, Goldsmith also made a cameo appearance.
[76] A description based on the handwritten sketch kept in Los Angeles' Margaret Herrick Library, saying 'Main Title Reel 1 part 3 (Theme from Basic Instinct)'.
[77] Mark Walker, *Basic Instinct*, in *Gramophone- Film Music Good Cd Guide*, Harrow, Gramophone Publications Limited, 1996, p.93.

transitional section, a theme refrain, a brief coda.

[*Basic Instinct*, main theme, p.1 (sheet)]

Cellos and basses in *pp* create a harmonic base (D minor), while harps
rise and fall on the tonic seventh chord; the violas show an *ostinato* figuration which is particularly effective as it rises and falls between *pp*
and *mf*; at the beginning, a – possibly electronic – percussive instrument (indicated on the orchestral sketch as: 'dso #62 chase on') ex-
ecutes an A note (dominant in this tone) in *p*, which becomes less and
less intense until the start of the following third bar, picking up again

54

and repeating this pattern during the first six bars; this instrument is heard again when the main theme is refrained. Clarinets enter at b.3 and, together with the b.4 violins, create the first section of the theme enunciation; the scheme is repeated in the following bars, though with a change in woods: flutes at b.5; flutes, oboes and clarinets at b.9. The woodwind crescendo is the enunciation's strong suit, together with the decrease of violins in the following one. The ethereal instrumentation of the MAIN TITLE theme, along with its rhythmic regularity, contribute to the creation of a tranquil sound conveying a sense of wait and dread. In this sense, it is a *thriller* score overcoming the boundaries of its own genre (and its own movie):

> An exceptional, complicated, sensual, violent and instinctual score, where Goldsmith recalls his own education rooted in the style of Herrmann and translates in sound the morbid universe of *eros* and *thanatos* created by Verhoeven. Two themes: the first one (MAIN TITLE) emerges from a series of suggestive and repetitive chords, with underlining electronic effects and an obsessive use of woodwinds; the second one (CROSSED LEGS, NIGHT LIFE), executed by violins, has a dynamic and supportive function, an unsettling exercise in counterpoint and rhythmic violence. Alexander Courage's orchestration underlines Goldsmith's harsher textures, a return to the American composer's roots: or, rather, a return to a high and bold expressive "temperature" marking some of his best scores from the '60s and '70s.[78]

A "thrilling" score, therefore, not only in its percussive and violent passages, but especially when taking a lulling and undulating rhythm (such as in the MAIN TITLE), exploiting the movie's darker *film noir* nature: the plot's ambiguity is highlighted by a repetition of the main theme at the end, after the piece accompanying the final credits.

Though Courage was a fine orchestrator, who had honed his craft through years of practice, we can suppose his contribution to this score

---

[78] ROBERTO PUGLIESE, *Basic instinct*, in "Segnocinema", n.57, September/October 1992, p.87. The CD currently on sale was published by Varèse Sarabande; later on a double unofficial CD and an authorized double CD pack – by Prometheus, a Belgian recording label connected to "Soundtrack!" magazine – were also published.

was limited to secondary details – as can also be inferred from the composer's handwritten sketch. His touch is apparent in scores in need of a higher orchestral skill, often more energetic and less personal than *Basic Instinct*'s. He might have contributed to other parts of this score, just as he did in more recent adventure movies and thrillers, which included several fast moments: *First Knight*, *The Mummy*, *The 13th Warrior* and the ending of *Hollow Man*.

After Courage's retirement (coinciding with his last movie with Verhoeven), Mark McKenzie, as we previously said, took on the role of orchestrating Goldsmith's last compositions. In Goldsmith's final years, the composer's timbric research moved on to less unconventional ensembles. An example of the post-Courage phase is given by the thriller *Along Came a Spider* (2001; directed by Lee Tamahori), and its orchestra of 16 violins I, 16 violins II, 12 violas, 11 cellos, 8 basses, 2 flutes, 2 clarinets, 2 oboes, 2 bassoons, 4 French horns, 3 trumpets, 3 trombones, 1 tuba, 4 percussionists, 2 harps and an electronic keyboard player – overall, a pretty traditional ensemble. On the same page is the score for *The Sum of All Fears* (2002; directed by Phil Alden Robinson), which also shows an operatic soprano *aria* during the opening credits, quite an unusual choice in Goldsmith's career. For *Looney Tunes- Back in Action* (2003; directed by Joe Dante), a peculiar example of interaction between real-life actors and cartoons (the latter being represented by the Warner Bros.' *Looney Tunes*) the traditional orchestra is joined by a guitar and an accordion; the fragmented result, reminiscent of the cartoons on which the movie is based, manages to highlight every instrument's timbre. With this last endeavor,[79] going above and beyond the requests of the studio, Goldsmith proved his great skill at musical parodies, created through the use of rhythmic fragmentation.

Be it Morton, Courage or McKenzie, the lines between a composer and his orchestrators are so blurred that trying to distinguish between contributions is an extremely complex feat. From a direct examination of Goldsmith's manuscripts, however, we tend to believe that the au-

---

[79] McKenzie also collaborated with Goldsmith on a movie score, for *Timeline*, which was replaced onscreen but later released on record.

thor always enjoyed complete orchestral independence, all the more justified by his abilities as a conductor.

* * *

Working relationship with directors

Collaborations between composers and directors, in spite of long-standing examples found even within the Hollywood industry,[80] are usually far from being a basic element of cinematic conception. The current working method, in production studios especially, is for the musician to start working after the movie has been edited, trying to reach the best technical result, rather than conceiving specific goals with screenwriters and directors during the early development of a project.

In Europe, artistic collaborations are more common, they can hardly be defined a veritable "parallel work". There are some examples – infrequent, though proof in themselves – of an "inverted procedure", when a director shoots certain sequences based on written music or in strict relation to sound, with the aim of creating a sort of rhythm, later enhanced during the editing phase. The most famous collaborations of this kind occurred between Italian director Sergio Leone and composer Ennio Morricone, – working together from 1964 to 1984 –[81] British director Peter Greenaway and composer Michael Nyman, as well as Polish director Krzysztof Kieslowski and composer Zbigniew Preisner.

More traditional, though remarkable in terms of expressive freedom and continuity, was the collaboration between American director Steven Spielberg and composer John Williams, as well as, in Italian movies, the artistic relationship between Federico Fellini and Nino

---

[80] Let it suffice to think of the cooperation between Blake Edwards and Henry Mancini, spanning more than 20 movies; between Michael Curtiz and Max Steiner, almost thirty movies; Henry King and Alfred Newman, who were just as prolific; and, more recently, between David Cronenberg and Howard Shore, or Joel e Ethan Coen and Carter Burwell.

[81] An additional chapter was never completed due to the director's death.

Rota, which became well-known in the movie industry and beyond. Less famous, though more musically "advanced", was the work of Michelangelo Antonioni with Giovanni Fusco.

Morricone and Leone, as per the composer's admission,[82] had known each other since youth and found themselves working together on *Per un pugno di dollari* (*A Fistful of Dollars*, 1964). Their working method developed almost exclusively from tunes created by Morricone, which the director used as a foundation to establish his shooting rhythm. The composer often created the music during the actual shooting of movies; the important thing was for him and the director to work in close contact, in order to produce a joint result.

The significant cooperation between Greenaway and Nyman, spanning from 1976 to 1991, started with short and medium features and was followed by a consistent (though not always very demanding) joint effort. This allowed them to create unique works that mixed Greenaway's self-described *mannerism* with Nyman's musical *minimalism*. The composer also brought to the director's attention a few pieces he had written with his previous Michael Nyman Band ensemble: from them Greenaway drew rhythm and iteration – a recurring feature of Nyman's music, even off-screen – in order to create visual shots inspired by paintings, especially those of Dutch master Jan Vermeer. Greenaway was less interested in the story he was telling and more in the shape of his sequences, and Nyman's music was often instrumental to this aim. Their professional relationship started with *Goole by Numbers* (1976), a medium-length film, and continued with a few minor works[83] leading up to their first feature, *The Draughtsman's Contract* (1982). For this movie, Nyman liberally drew inspiration from Henry Purcell's music, creating the score's structure from its melodic and

---

[82] SERGIO MICELI: *Il binomio Leone-Morricone. Nascita ed evoluzione di uno stile musicale*, in *Morricone, la musica...*, op.cit., p. 107-169. *See also* MASINA CARAVETTA, *Il western di Leone-Morricone*, in *La musica del cinema*, op.cit., p.135-159.

[83] The Nyman-Greenaway relationship includes nine medium-length films, three shorts, a composition of 99 shorts (*The Falls*, 1980) as well as five movies.

rhythmic cells.[84] This work helped Nyman set himself up as a "post-modern composer", a status he maintained during his cooperation with Greenaway and beyond. The main feature of *The Draughtsman's Contract*'s score is that the different pieces are independent from each other – in a later score, *Drowning by Numbers* (1988), every track was modeled on bars 21-26 and 58-61 of Mozart's *Sinfonia Concertante* K364's second movement. Between these two works came *A Zed and Two Noughts* (1982) as well as the only one of Greenaway's movies from this time that was not scored by Nyman: *The Belly of an Architect* (1987; its score consisted in an album by Belgian minimalist composer Wim Mertens, as well as in pieces by American composer Glenn Branca). The following movie, *The Cook, the Thief, His Wife and Her Lover* (1989) was a patchwork of music previously written for other, often mournful occasions. *Memorial*, in particular, had been composed by Nyman to commemorate the tragedy at Heysel stadium, where on May 29, 1985, 39 people died during a soccer championship final. The pieces match the movie's funereal atmosphere, culminating in an act of cannibalism. The relationship between the two artists ended with *Prospero's Books* (1991), a movie based on Shakespeare's *The Tempest*; everything seemed to proceed well, as Nyman wrote his most complex score yet for a Greenaway movie. Composer and director, however, were dissatisfied with their joint effort and decided to abruptly cut off their partnership – though their will to pursue new artistic routes also played a contributing factor in their decision. Soon after, Nyman was hired by New Zealander director Jane Campion to write a score for *The Piano* (1993). The composer followed the "Greenaway procedure" in the sense that he provided the music – namely, the piano pieces performed by the main character (Holly Hunter) – before the movie was shot. Sur-

---

[84] Nyman, on his first movie, tried his hand at a sort of "Purcell-like" exercise – he knew Purcell well from his own musicology degree with Thurston Dart, who had published editions of Purcell's music. With this movie, Greenaway believed he had achieved the best fusion of image and music; quot. in: Giovanni Bogani, *Peter Greenaway*, Milan, Il Castoro, 1995, p.12. The same book mentions a simple yet programmatic statement, a "manifesto" of sorts given by the director:: 'In this movie, music and images have equal rights'(*Ibid*.).

prisingly, this soundtrack became a bestseller and made the composer very famous, a rare instance even for the most celebrated names in the movie-scoring world. Since then the musician was hired by other directors and, every so often, summoned to Hollywood, where unfortunately he did not reach the desired success, mainly due to the fact that the studio system allowed him little freedom.

Another professional relationship creating an unusual, brave and creative interaction between drama and music was born between Polish artists Kieslowski and Preisner. The director's untimely demise, however, put an end to a collaboration which would otherwise have produced more relevant results. Kieslowski and Preisner's common path was marked by the following works: the two *Dekalog* medium-length movies (1988-89, *English Title: The Decalogue*), *La Double Vie de Véronique* (1991; *The Double Life of Veronique*), the trilogy formed by *Trois Couleurs: Bleu* (1993), *Trois Couleurs: Blanc* (1994) and *Trois Couleurs: Rouge* (1994), as well as the earlier, musically less significant *Bez Konca* (1984; *Without End*). The script for the first episode in Kieslowski's French-flag movie trilogy – each of the works representing the director's take on the issues of liberty, equality and fraternity – was conceived around the score, a supposed *Concert for European Unification*. The main character's husband, a composer working on this very concert, dies in a car crash before managing to finish it. During the course of the movie we can hear fragments of this *cantata* – its lyrics coming from the 13th verse of Saint Paul's Letter to the Corinthians[85] – one after the other, as the work is completed and finally played at the end. The main character herself (Juliette Binoche), together with a colleague of her husband's, "feels" the music she is working on, while the spectator participates in this unusual work in progress, the likes of which have rarely been seen in movies:

> De Corsy-Van Den Budenmayer-Preisner's solemn music has the complex task of conveying the movie's "Pauline" and "European" message, a *pars*

---

[85]   As highlighted in Serafino Murri, *Krzysztof Kieslowski*, Milan, Il Castoro, 1996, p.142: 'this is one of the few biblical texts not mentioning God', a fact resonating with Kieslowski's wider nonreligious views.

costruens to Kieslowski's harsh criticism of show business, as well as aiding the movie's organic expression and joining its cinematic *rhythm* until it becomes a sort of direction to the score: this might be noticed in the scenes of discussion about the Concert's instrumentation, where we can see and hear the musical variations on the sheet while Julie and Olivier are talking.[86]

In his previous endeavor – *La Double Vie de Véronique* – Preisner had also come to the forefront by providing the *cantata* sung with a choir by the main character (Irène Jacob, starring in the double role of Véronique and Veronika), "smuggling it in" as a piece by imaginary composer Van Den Budenmayer[87] (in this instance the lyrics were from the second *canto* of Dante Alighieri's *Paradiso*), which the composer had already used in some parts of his *Dekalog* score.

The professional relationship between Spielberg and Williams, on the other hand, started with the director's second movie, *The Sugarland Express* (1973). Williams, originally from New York, worked on all of Spielberg's following pictures, with the exception of his 1983 *Twilight Zone - The Movie* episode (scored by Jerry Goldsmith) and of 1985's *The Color Purple*, which, being connected to African-American tradition, had its score coordinated by Quincy Jones. We might say that, with the exception of the *Star Wars* series, Williams found his utmost freedom and satisfaction in the technological fairy tales created by the Cincinnati-born director. A few examples of their memorable partnership are: *Jaws* (1975); *Close Encounters of the Third Kind* (1977); *1941* (1979); the four movies featuring adventurer-archaeologist Indiana Jones: *Raiders of the Lost Ark* (1981), *Indiana Jones and the Temple of Doom* (1984), *Indiana Jones and the Last Crusade* (1989), *Indiana Jones and the Kingdom of the Crystal Skull* (2008); as well as: *E.T.* (1982), *Empire of the Sun* (1987), *Always* (1990), *Jurassic Park* (1993), *Schindler's List* (1993), *Amistad* (1997), *Saving Private Ryan* (1998),

---

[86]   MURRI, *op.cit.*, p.149. the passage in question can be heard in the music's recording, *Trois Couleurs: Bleu*, cd Virgin 72438 39027-2, especially piece #19 'Olivier and Julie – Trial Composition'.

[87]   This imaginary composer was supposedly Dutch and from the 18th century. This 'game' probably aims to provide a sort of "musicological justification" to Preisner's composition.

A.I. (2000), *Minority Report* (2002), *Catch Me If You Can* (2002), *The Terminal* (2004), *Munich* (2005), *War of the Worlds* (2005), *Lincoln* (2012).

Save for a few works with other directors – Oliver Stone was among them – John Williams found his most becoming artistic expression within the Lucas-Spielberg production system; he thus reached, so to speak, a working tranquility that Goldsmith had always struggled to obtain. The comparison between Williams and Goldsmith, often made due to their common experience and ability, highlights a few basic differences in their approach: while the former almost invariably chose high-level productions and overall "high-quality" movies, as well as establishing stable working relationships with directors, – Spielberg, Chris Columbus, Oliver Stones' two "presidential" movies *JFK* (1991) and *Nixon* (1995) as well as *Born on the Fourth of July* (1989) – the latter often showcased the best of his craft on movies that were not particularly gratifying from an aesthetic point of view, and was fond of highlighting less "poetic" sequences. Moreover, except for his frequent partnerships with Franklin J. Schaffner, Joe Dante and the less relevant Fred Schepisi, Goldsmith never maintained a significant number of stable working relationships with directors.

Sometimes, in European cinema especially, a director and a musician start a professional or personal relationship leading to a close, almost symbiotic working method. One The aforementioned Fellini-Rota relationship is one such example – some of their most memorable titles being *La strada* (1954), *La dolce vita* (1959), *8 ½* (1963), *Roma* (1972), *Casanova* (1975), *Orchestra Rehearsal* (1979); Sergio Miceli summarizes their artistic union in a chapter of his monography about the relationship between music and movies.[88]

Other profitable and long-term relationships can be found between German scriptwriter and director Rainer Werner Fassbinder and composer Peer Raben,[89] as well as between French writer-director Alain Robbe-Grillet and Michel Fano, a sound technician who later started

---

[88] Miceli, *Il sodalizio Rota-Fellini. Una breve analisi*, in *Musica e cinema...*, op.cit., p.385-404.

[89] Together they worked on a few theatrical works and, among others, on movies like *Chinese Roulette* (1976), *The Marriage of Maria Braun* (1978), *Veronika Voss* (1982), *Querelle* (1982).

creating purely musical sounds. Both relationships were born in the literary and psychological "art house" film world, where the scores aimed to help the authors (both, incidentally, literary figures: Fassbinder was a playwright, Robbe-Grillet a novelist from the so-called *nouveau roman* genre) achieve their results. Of a less intellectual (not to say more superficial) tone is the close collaboration between French director Claude Lelouch and his trusty composer Francis Lai, who provided him with catchy, almost pop-sounding tunes; Lai became famous in the U.S. as well, after winning an Oscar for *Love Story* (1970; directed by Arthur Hiller); the professional relationship between Lelouch and Lai lasted for more than twenty movies, mirroring the two artists' "light" notion of feelings and of their reflection in music.[90]

In American movies in general, and within the major studio system in particular, it is customary for directors to hire different professionals who are under contract with the same studio. This results in less freedom of collaboration, as well as in composers developing a fundamental spirit of adaptation . Despite a few exceptions it is hard to imagine, within the U.S. "industry", a kind of interactive union between a director and a composer like the one existing between Kieslowski and Preisner; the director, at best, might allow a composer with a sufficiently strong contract the freedom to write the music he feels is most suited to the movie: an emblematic example in this sense is given by Howard Shore's music for David Cronenberg's movies.[91] The relationship between Shore and Cronenberg, both Canadians, began in 1979 with *The Brood* and was initially limited to horror movies, albeit of significant quality. The use of an unsettling (though not excessively cutting-edge) musical language was Shore's trademark, especially noticeable in *The Fly* (1985) and *Dead Ringers* (1988). Using the style he had created for Cronenberg's movies, Shore also scored the mystic-philosophical thrill-

---

[90] Their most famous work was *Un homme et une femme* (1966; *A Man and a Woman*), the structure of which was then repeated in other films; the movie's main theme also became very famous.

[91] Later on, as we already said, Shore delved into the score of J.R.R. Tolkien's saga, for which he chose a more accessible language with strong recurrent motives.

er *Se7en* (1995; directed by David Fincher).

More traditional, though no less groundbreaking, was the collaboration between Alfred Hitchcock and Bernard Herrmann, perhaps the most famous of its kind in American movies. Hitchcock and Herrmann worked together on eight movies, plus the one that caused their break-up; their debut with *The Trouble with Harry* (1955) was followed by *The Wrong Man* (1956), *The Man Who Knew Too Much* (1956), *Vertigo* (1958), *North by Northwest* (1959), *Psycho* (1960), *The Birds* (1963; where Herrmann, in lieu of composing original music, oversaw the sound effects) and *Marnie* (1964). The score for *Torn Curtain* (1966), though fully composed, did not meet the director's requirements, so much that Hitchcock replaced it with a totally new one written by John Addison.[92]

A less emphatic collaboration occurred between Sam Peckinpah, a "disruptive" American director working from the late '60s to the following decade, and composer Jerry Fielding: their joint efforts created such classics as *The Wild Bunch* (1969), *Straw Dogs* (1971), *Junior Bonner* (1972), a 1972 score for *The Getaway* which was rejected by the production team and replaced with music by Quincy Jones, *Bring Me the Head of Alfredo Garcia* (1974) and *The Killer Elite* (1977). Peckinpah was especially devoted to the musical side of his work, though he often had trouble with producers, especially at the start of his career, because he insisted on imposing his own editing choices. Goldsmith worked with him on *The Ballad of Cable Hogue* (1970), squeezing himself between the director's first and second collaboration with Fielding. Smaller in importance but extraordinary in continuity was the collaboration between Blake Edwards and Italian-American composer Henry Mancini, resulting, between 1957 and 1993, in about thirty movies including the *The Pink Panther* series (1964) as well as *Breakfast at Tiffany's* (1961), *The Party* (1968) and *Victor Victoria* (1982). Mancini's music was often "lighter" and rich in jazz and swing elements. Once more, Goldsmith set himself between Edwards and Mancini by creating the score for *Wild Rovers* (1971), a melancholy Western which (not coincidentally)

---

[92] The *Torn Curtain* case opened the way to the "rejected scores" issue, which later became more and more frequent.

represented a departure from the director's usual carefree style.

Within a very different production context it is worth highlighting the relationship between music and Japanese cinema. While composers such as Tōru Takemitsu (1930-96) worked consistently in movies without tarnishing their artistic merit, other, less advanced musicians worked extensively and almost exclusively in movies; such is the case with Masaru Satō, who played an important role in the movies by Japanese director Akira Kurosawa. Kurosawa, perhaps the best-known Japanese author in the West, gave his musicians an often fundamental role by specializing in epic adventures. The relationship between Kurosawa and Satō started with the death of the director's favorite composer, Fumio Hayasaka, who had scored eight of Kurosawa's movies. After completing Hayasaka's work on *Ikomono no kiroku* (1955; *I Live in Fear*), Satō debuted with Kurosawa's *Kumonosu-jo* (1957; *Throne of Blood;* a sort of Japanese *Macbeth*), working on the following eight movies until 1965, the year of *Akahige* (*Red Beard*). Satō's language combined the popular vein – these were the years of Kurosawa's picaresque movies, such as *The Hidden Fortress* (1958) – with his country's "cultured" tradition. *Red Beard* marked the end of their collaboration;[93] five years later, Kurosawa shot *Dodes'kaden* (1970), scored by Takemitsu, though the result was misunderstood by audience and critics alike. Later on, Takemitsu worked with Kurosawa again on *Ran* (1985), the Japanese maestro's *King Lear*.

Widespread emigration from Europe in the first half of the 20th century meant that several Austrian-German artists of Jewish descent started working for American studios. A strong spirit of solidarity was born among directors and composers who had been forced to flee their native lands; this was especially true at Warner Brothers where, starting in the 1930s, an extensive season of adventure and *noir* movies began,

---

[93] *Red Beard* was Kurosawa's turning point, as it closed a phase marked not only by the director's relationship with this musician, but also with his favorite actor, Tōshiro Mifune. The Kurosawa-Satō relationship occurred roughly at the same time as the one between Hitchcock and Herrmann, which started on the same year and ended one year later.

reaching significant results. This period (lasting until the first half of the 1940s) saw the development of a collaboration between Michael Curtiz, a Hungarian-American director, and two of the most important Hollywood composers of his time: Erich Wolfgang Korngold and Max Steiner. The Curtiz/Korngold artistic collaboration created *Captain Blood* (1936), *The Adventures of Robin Hood* (1938), *The Sea Hawk* (1940), *The Sea Wolf* (1941) – adventurous movies with little psychological depth forming the first great vein of Korngold's work in Hollywood (the second was drama, represented by his work with Irving Rapper, Sam Wood and Curtis Bernhardt). More consistent was the professional relationship between Curtiz and Steiner, spanning several decades for a total of twenty-seven works: the most famous among them was *Casablanca* (1942), where the musician showcased a knack for use of vintage tunes, though he also fell for the hackneyed cliché of employing *La Marseillaise* in connection to a French setting (in this case, the French colony of Morocco); other examples were *The Charge of the Light Brigade* (1936) and *Angels with Dirty Faces* (1938). Steiner also built a privileged relationship with John Ford, joining him on few but significant works such as *The Informer* (1935) and *The Searchers* (1956).

Goldsmith's attitude towards directors was ambivalent: on the one hand he enjoyed some stable, significant and "heartfelt" collaborations, though they were never particularly extensive: on the other, he forged relationships with less-talented directors, often resulting from a mere coincidence in production. The first kind is exemplified by the relationship between Goldsmith and Franklin J. Schaffner (going from 1963 to 1986, although in the meantime the director also worked with other composers) or fantasy and comedy director Joe Dante (starting in 1983 and ending with the composer's last musical work in 2003). It was not unusual for such intense professional relationships to be marked by a human component, as well as by professional esteem, thus becoming a friendship of sorts. This is especially true of Schaffner, a contemporary of Goldsmith's, as we may notice from the audio commentary included in a DVD edition of *Planet of the Apes*. The second kind of collaboration occurred with such directors as Fred Schepisi, who worked with Goldsmith on five movies; Michael Crichton, Gordon Douglas, Tom Gries and Jack Lee Thompson, four movies each; Boris Sagal, George Pan Cosmatos, Richard Fleischer (three movies each), and so forth. These directors were usually good camera technicians rather than "authors" in a European sense (except for Crichton, who was also a writer). As paradoxical as it may sound, Goldsmith's most significant collaborations happened with the directors he met less frequently. He reached excellent results with Dutch director Paul Verhoeven on three separate occasions. At different times we find him working with Robert Wise on two rather demanding movies: *The Sand Pebbles* (1966) and *Star Trek: The Motion Picture* (1979); in this case, as well, the rarity of their collaborations is matched by a high level of quality.[94]

Goldsmith's relationship with Verhoeven, as we said, resulted in an excellent quality of work. The Dutch director started his career at the beginning of the 1960s and, after about ten movies and a few TV shows, landed his first American production in 1985. From a musical point of view, Verhoeven's Hollywood experience was split between two names: Goldsmith and Basil Poledouris. The latter, a composer of Greek background, was thrust into the spotlight by his symphonic score for *Conan the Barbarian* (1982; directed by John Milius), as well as other symphonic works he composed for adventure and epic movies. Verhoeven used Poledouris' scores on his most patriotic endeavors, such as *Flesh & Blood* (1985), *Robocop* (1987) and *Starship Troopers* (1997). Critics highlighted the Dutch director's favorite and recurring themes: misogyny, sex, violence. Verhoeven's collaboration with Goldsmith, on *Total Recall*, – based on a Philip K. Dick short story – includes a considerable amount of action music, as the movie has very few dull moments. The uninterrupted dynamic "push" provided by Goldsmith's score favors a certain rhythm in editing, arranging characters like pawns in an unstoppable rush of escape; so much that *Total Recall* looks more like an action movie than a futuristic story partly set on Mars. The movie

---

[94] Wise was a well-known name in Hollywood; he edited Orson Welles' *Citizen Kane* (1941) before becoming a good director himself: *Executive Suite* (1954) and *West Side Story* (1961) are two of his works worth mentioning.

rarely slows down, except at the end, when the main character (played by Arnold Schwarzenegger) and the girl who helped him join the rebellion against the political and financial regime (Rachel Ticotin) envision a future of apparent peace; this is the only part where Goldsmith finally allows for a melodic coda sustained by less energetic harmonies. Before *Total Recall*, the composer had often provided scores for chase sequences, such as in *The Wind and the Lion* (1975; the track RAISULI ATTACKS), *Capricorn One* (1978; the track BREAKOUT), *Alien* (1979; the track BREAKAWAY), *Outland* (1981; HOT WATER and THE HUNTED). In this sense, we might say he effectively managed to create a "rhythmic handbook" for action movies. In *Total Recall*'s MAIN TITLE, the rhythmic and percussive charge is already acting as a pulsating engine, highlighting the movie's futuristic tone. Goldsmith wrote every musical piece appearing in the movie, even the brief TV commercials populating the underground sequences at the beginning, as well as the short background track *Divertimento in D*. Goldsmith briefly recalled his first experiences with Verhoeven and his working relationship with the director:

> What makes it so interesting is that Paul Verhoeven makes his characters so appealing. He takes a relatively ordinary story and deepens, to make less obvious characters. The public can realize it or not (...) but he shall transmit it and I get it. (...) We met when we did *Total Recall*. I was a great admirer of Paul's Dutch films, especially *Soldier of Orange* and *Spetters*. Even *Robocop* is a real hoot. I've seen his trademark, some hidden kind of humor that knows how to put these comic-book stories. We had a great relationship during *Total Recall*. (...) Since he could not come to recording sessions, I was creating so-called *electronic mock ups* of music. Thanks to computer and electronic equipment, I was able, once written, to record music on a computer and listen to it in sync with the video through a simulation of the orchestra. Therefore Paul had the opportunity to preview how the outcome would be. An interesting side of him that I noticed is that he saw the scenes several times with the music, and after he made a few comments. I can remember how in that movie he liked everything I did, to the point that he often asked to listen the isolated music track. It was the beginning of a very good collaboration.[95]

---

[95]   Transcription of Jerry Goldsmith's commentary on the *Hollow Man* DVD, chapter 2.

Their second movie together, *Basic Instinct* – which we have already mentioned when referring to orchestration – proved more difficult. The story is about a detective plagued by several personal issues (played by Michael Douglas), investigating on a murder case. The main suspect in the murder is the deceased's lover, a writer played by Sharon Stone, who ensnares the detective in a perverted relationship. The movie caused much controversy, upon its release, due to its explicit sex scenes and a certain misogynistic tone, which the critics pinpointed as the core of Verhoeven's "poetics". Goldsmith approached the picture by giving due consideration to its brief action sequences, while at the same time underlining the ambiguity of the two protagonists and of the equally perverted and disturbed supporting characters. About his work on this movie, the composer himself recalled:

> *Basic Instinct (...)* is a very complex picture. It was a murder mystery, a love story or a thriller? Or all these things together? Paul Verhoeven had a very clear idea of who these people were, what he wanted and how he wanted it. The difficulty with the music, is to translate the emotion and drama to make it musically. Music is in my view something as abstract: A painter can say that something is red or blue, the association has existed for so long with colors so we understand it, it will be difficult to imagine the various shades, but we have a general idea. But in music this is difficult to implement. And [this film] became a real tug of war, because whatever I did, to try to find a common denominator, the theme, a musical motif identifier that encapsulates all that and roughly the essence of the film and characters, I could not define it. (...) Verhoeven pushed me in the search, and finally, after several attempts, I found the right tone for the theme that became one of the two that structure the film.[96]

Eight years later, the two professionals met again for their third collaboration, *Hollow Man*. In the meantime, Verhoeven had directed two more pictures, a less successful one (*Showgirls*, 1995) for which he had not

---

[96]   Transcription, *op.cit.*, chapters 2 & 3.

needed a very sophisticated score,[97] and another one chock-full of war action, based on science fiction master Robert Heinlein's novel *Starship Troopers* (1997), for which, ten years after *Robocop* (1987), he went back to working with Poledouris. The Greek composer thus proved himself capable of creating pulsating and forceful rhythms for two clearly patriotic movies. In *Hollow Man*, Verhoeven approached the theme of invisibility by considering all the nefarious and perverted consequence of this futuristic possibility, while leaving out the often humorous tones of various other movies on this topic, from genre progenitor *The Invisible Man* (1933; directed by James Whale) and its sequels, to the more recent *Memoirs of an Invisible Man* (1992; directed by John Carpenter). Here's the composer's comment on his experience with this movie:

> [Paul Verhoeven] had made sure that since the picture has announced I was hired for the music. There was not yet a cast, and it lacked a year and a half at the beginning of filming. (...) The film is not about violence [essentially] but a man who sells his soul to the devil: it is a tragedy, a brilliant mind gone astray, and his theme, [that is heard in the opening credits], is nostalgic. With him I wanted to convey a sense of impending disaster.[98]

The most important musical parts of this movie, except for the theme exposition and its varied repetitions, is represented by the three transformations occurring in the first part of the story, as well as the final sequence showing the invisible man Sebastian (Kevin Bacon) slaughtering his colleagues, and the main character's demise caused by his love interest, Linda (Elisabeth Shue). About the transformation scenes,

> I worried because they were three and many [visual] elements were repetitive. [The first, when the gorilla Isabelle becomes visible again], begins with a mechanical tune, then takes over the main theme for Sebastian, the sudden section of suspense and suddenly we have the resolution. Ver-

---

97 Despite the director's usual collaboration with Goldsmith or Poledouris, the score for this less-than-successful movie was entrusted to former Eurythmics member David Stewart, who was more in tune with the film's *disco* atmosphere.

98 Transcription, *op.cit.*, chapters 1 & 3.

hoeven was very excited to listen to the 'return music' of Isabelle. It had become a very spiritual thing, that you were talking about the right to do such a thing, bring back to life a living being. At the same time in the lab there was always a kind of tedium mechanical rhythms incessant testing, the triumphs and failures [and this had to stand in the music].[99]

The transformation scenes, therefore, show a recurring solemn motif, due to the almost mystical approach suggested by the director. Musically speaking, the scenes undergo several changes in tempo (6/8, 5/8) as well as presenting a *pizzicato* figuration. The final sequence is a veritable musical *tour de force*, pure visual action underlined by percussive music. Out of the movie's last 29 minutes, which include the final credits and the repetition of the opening credits' 'Sebastian's theme', 27 and a half are of music and very few of dialogue. About these sequences, the composer himself admitted:

> There aren't subtleties here. With this type of action, you have to do the 'booms' of the case when there is a corpse. But [from here] he began his murderous rampage and gradually he removed all of them. I tried to give the feeling that the others are organizing to defend themselves. The theme for the laboratory, which is associated to the character of Linda, in these sequences, becomes heroic.[100]

Among directors of proven ability and inspiration, the composer's collaboration with Ridley Scott, a British expatriate in Hollywood, was paradoxical: the author of *Blade Runner* crossed paths with Goldsmith on two occasions: *Alien* and *Legend*, both presenting their fair share of problems in relation to the score's reception. In *Alien*, perhaps one of Goldsmith's most interesting scores, some pieces were replaced because considered unfit to the mood envisioned by the director; as a consequence, the corresponding scenes took on an almost opposite meaning. Even worse was Goldsmith's *Legend* experience: the American version of the movie was released with an entirely new score writ-

---

[99] Transcription, *op.cit.*, chapters 3 & 4.
[100] Transcription, *op.cit.*, chapter 20.

ten by another composer, although Goldsmith's music continued to circulate on the European version of the film.

Goldsmith's professional relationship with Richard Donner was very different and mainly connected to a single movie, *The Omen* (1976), which earned the composer his first and only Academy Award. Goldsmith received the Oscar for *Best Original Score* on May 28, 1977, beating two nominated scores by Bernard Herrmann (*Obsession* and *Taxi Driver*). It is quite unusual to notice how such a good score did not result in further collaborations with this director – though Goldsmith wrote the music for other movies, shot by different directors, completing the *The Omen* saga. It is worth mentioning, however, that on his following movie *Superman* (1978), Donner chose to work with John Williams (whose *score* became one of the best-known in movie history), and he later started successful collaborations with other musicians such as Michael Kamen, Carter Burwell and Hans Zimmer. For *The Omen*, Goldsmith was free to compose without excessive pressure; the only request from the director in terms of scoring, the musician recalls, was based on a simple ploy to convey the mounting tension in the plot. An example is given by the scene where the young protagonist, who is the embodiment of the anti-Christ, is going to church with his parents. The piece, Broken Vows, is based on an *ostinato* ploy. As the composer said:

> *Jaws* [1975; directed by Steven Spielberg, *a/n*] had just come out and there was this very effective *ostinato* that John [Williams] wrote (...). It puts this tremendous energy to it. It was very effective in a simple way. Dick [Richard Donner] was very impressed with that because it pushed the film. The important function of music is to help rhythm sometimes, adding extra energy to the film. That's about the only thing he really discussed with me. I was in Los Angeles and he called me from London. He said he had just seen *Jaws*, he liked that feeling. He wanted something like that for his movie, some strong rhythmic idea, that started simple and became more and more intense.[101]

---

[101] Transcription of Jerry Goldsmith's commentary on the DVD boxed set extras for *The Omen Trilogy, 25° anniversary edition*, 20th Century-Fox Home Entertainment Inc., 2001. The CD was published by Varèse Sarabande; vsd-6288, 2001.

This cycle, besides the traditional orchestral ensemble, was provided by a "satanic" choir – a brutal presence that was meant to be musically ironic – accompanying the three movies in an almost parodistic way, both by singing and simply making noise. The closest reference we can pinpoint, considering the importance of rhythm in this track, is Igor Stravinsky's *fauve period* (about halfway through THE KILLER STORM, a piece for choir and orchestra, where we find a string pace similar to the beginning of *Les Augures Printaniers: Danses des Adolescentes* from the first part of *Le Sacre du Printemps*) as well as a certain influence from late-Romantic tradition, namely in the massive use of chromatism (especially clear in the saga's third movie, *The Final Conflict*, 1980). Of the first *The Omen* movie, Goldsmith remembers:

> The whole picture allowed me to do... I don't mean avant-garde, but some freedom musically, pushing some more avant-garde style since I had done *Planet of the Apes* ten or nine years previous. Maybe those two [*Planet of the Apes* and *The Omen*] are the most avant-garde for me, for film music, that I've ever done. Not that I haven't dared in others, but I had less chances. That's why I liked it, [because] it gave me the power really to do that I wanted to do.[102]

The references to avant-garde style, noticeable in various parts of the trilogy, are well represented by the piece called THE DOGS ATTACK, accompanying the scene[103] where ambassador Thorn (Gregory Peck) and a photographer (David Warner) are attacked by satanic dogs while looking for evidence in a graveyard. Goldsmith recalls the sequence, highlighting the fact that, at the time, he'd had the means to fully reach his goal:

> In THE DOGS ATTACK there are some interesting things. The chorus is not singing, but making groans and strange noises, not necessarily music, but I incorporated they like music. Then interesting effects with the orchestra. Looking the picture again, if it was done today the recording could be

---

[102] Transcription, *op.cit.*
[103] The scene is in chapter 13 of the *The Omen* DVD.

much better, the dubbing could be much better. The orchestra could be twice as big, the choir also twice as big. We knew the budget was very limited on this film and maybe is [the reason] it's so good. Sometimes the absence of money pushes the imagination to work harder. Anyway, that scene really allowed me a lot of [freedom]. A slow building up becomes a terrifying scene.[104]

For this score, quite by chance, Goldsmith also wrote a song – a rather ordinary request on the production team's part, often complied before without a great display of creativity – by employing the tranquil and melodic tune appearing in one of the movie's first scenes.[105] The composer himself described its creation:

> Lee Remick and Gregory Peck are walking in the countryside and the theme is very pretty, it's very bucolic and lovely (...) That's one of the few romantic moments in the film (...). In the next scene the child is missing and they thought that something happened to their child. [track in the cd: WHERE IS HE?, a/n]. The he reappears, he's OK and the theme came back in full 'Hollywood' glory. Harvey [Harvey Bernhard] and Dick [Richard Donner] liked the theme so much. I wrote the theme in song shape, so they asked to write some lyrics for this. My wife Carol is a songwriter, so she wrote the lyrics. We recorded it along with the score for the album. There was a chorus, but it was very corny. We went on the mixing with the orchestral tracks and tried with different vocal groups, but it sounded always corny. The song and the arrangements sounded lousy. During that debate Carol was in the studio ticking the piano and singing and the microphones were on. The mixer, I and the producer of the album watched each other and we said: "Why not?". So we asked Carol to listen this and sing. We started the track and recorded it. She didn't know that we recorded, but we did it! And in the album went Carol's singing.[106]

Goldsmith's participation to the *The Omen* saga continued with *Damien: The Omen II* (1978; directed by Don Taylor) ending with *The Final Conflict* (1980; directed by Graham Baker); a fourth chapter was later added to

---

[104] Transcription, *op.cit.*
[105] The scene is in chapter 4 of the *The Omen* DVD.
[106] Transcription, *op.cit.*

the series and, in 2006, a remake of the original movie, scored by Marco Beltrami, paid homage to Goldsmith's music. A few decades after *The Omen*, in 2002, Donner and Goldsmith were supposed to work together again on *Timeline*, due to open the following year. The music had actually been composed and recorded but, for production reasons, it was later replaced with a score by up-and-coming composer Brian Tyler.[107] The *Timeline* score issue was quite controversial and revealed the extreme precariousness often surrounding the work of movie composers. Donner briefly recounts how:

> [Goldsmith] little by little played [the score] for us. I loved it, it was just great. Then I laid it up to the picture for the first time and I realized that I had really fucked up, that I was really hurting the picture.[108]

Due to the illness that would later lead to his death, Goldsmith was unable to write another score; the producers, therefore, took the practical decision of hiring a different composer. Goldsmith's relationship with Donner did not proceed beyond their first movie together, but the fact remains that the *Omen* score was significant and that, when recorded, it proved to have a life of its own.

---

[107] About the rejected scores issue, *see.* Appendix.

[108] RUDY KOPPL, *Interview with Richard Donner*, in "Music from the Movies", no. 41, January 2004, p.13. This issue includes a whole dossier on the *Timeline* movie score composition, referring to both Goldsmith's and Tyler's scores.

3
CROSSING MOVIE GENRES

Science fiction and fantasy

Goldsmith's science fiction work mainly consists in his participation to five of the *Star Trek* movies - which will be further analyzed in chapter 4 - though he also contributed to many other important movies pertaining to this genre, especially *Planet of the Apes* and *Alien.*

Here is how the composer himself described his approach to this cinematic genre:

> With science-fiction films, I'm interested in going back to my early days in television, [when I made some episodes of the TV series] *The Twilight Zone.* (...) I like doing those kinds of pictures because there was such great imagination going into the stories. They gave me, as a composer, a broad palette. I could do what I wanted to do. I think as far as me writing in a more avant-garde style, that culminated in *Planet of the Apes*, where I could pull out all the stops and do what I wanted. The more interesting and more far out I was going, the more experimental it was, the happier the director was. I had a free hand in that. Then I did *Logan's Run* and *Alien.* I guess a lot of movies.[109]

Goldsmith's score for *Planet of the Apes* can be compared to his earlier work on *Freud* (1962) for its use of an avant-garde musical language that was far from the stereotypes of the time. Before then, science fic-

---

[109] Transcription from Goldsmith's audio commentary to the DVD release of *Star Trek: The Motion Picture- Director's Edition*, Paramount Pictures, chapter 1.

tion movies had mostly chosen atmospheres of suspense, such as those found in Bernard Herrmann's score for *The Day the Earth Stood Still* (1951; directed by Robert Wise); in Goldsmith's case, however, the composer's musical research led him to use timbric parameters in a way that had never before been attempted in movie scoring.

While working for the Hollywood industry, Goldsmith, as many other cutting-edge musicians of his time, always had to deal with censorship of a more or less explicit kind. Music, being considered a mere "filler", had a better chance to escape the grip of censorship than any other part of a cinematic work, such as its plot or its topics. The '60s had brought about a strong desire for novelty, for experimentation, though the pioneers of movie scoring had already started experimenting a decade earlier. Alex North's score for *A Streetcar Named Desire* (1951; directed by Elia Kazan and based on a Tennessee Williams play) as well as Leonard Rosenman's score for *The Cobweb* (1955; directed by Vincent Minnelli) are two remarkable examples in this sense. The latter in particular adopted an avant-garde musical style with a complex and innovative language, atonal though not strictly serial, rarely employed in Hollywood movies and, until then, hardly ever found in movie scoring in general. North's score, on the other hand, paved the way for a much-imitated style by unabashedly applying a musical structure close to jazz to Kazan's dramatic images. However, while North also created more "ordinary" scores, reaching good results in big-budget historical movies such as *Spartacus* (1960) and *Cleopatra* (1963), Rosenman was more consistent with his own musical language, and always kept a low profile while trying to use his scarce movie work as a musical research ground. Both musicians, together with Bernard Herrmann, were for Goldsmith role models of sorts; though the composer, during the course of his career, came closer to emulating Rosenman's style, and always maintained a sporadic and not very meaningful relationship with jazz.

Goldsmith's approach to science fiction movies was guided by two main principles: the first one was to write music with a *reminiscence structure*, its themes returning in the course of a movie – or a saga, such as *Star Trek* – with a different sound each time, according to the situation on the screen and following the movie's dramatic development; the second one was to highlight the movie's atmosphere, which meant the score would be structured in short thematic, harmonic or rhythmic cells, not necessarily connected to a specific character, situation or place. The cells were then mashed together in such a way that, most of the time, the music appeared disconnected to the images it was written for. This sometimes resulted in an impression of monotony and "lack of center", but disconcerting the listener was the composer's exact purpose. Goldsmith used this method in a few, fairly successful science-fiction movies. One of them was *Planet of the Apes*, a benchmark – even in a strictly musical sense – of the composer's career. Two more scores showing a similar composing method, but with very different musical results, were written in close succession to one another: *Alien* (1979) and *Outland* (1981; directed by Peter Hyams). The first was a contemporary of *Star Trek: The Motion Picture*, though in terms of musical language, except for a few secondary passages, it might be considered its polar opposite. The three scores, with their distinct but similar styles, were part of a less glitzy musical narration: they managed to create a "suffocating" world of sounds, aiming to evoke a sense of anxiety and uncertainty. Rather than being plot-driven, the so-called *atmosphere* scores faced the audience with the psychological condition of the movie's situation and characters. The plot of more "earthly" science-fiction sagas such as *Star Wars* and *Star Trek* – where the outer-space setting is a mere metaphor – is usually marked by an epic and mythical element. The other kind of sci-fi movies, following the lead of *Planet of the Apes*, give the characters have little to no way of escaping their troubles, leaving them stranded in a hostile world that they are unable to understand, much less dominate.

Goldsmith thus created three difficult scores which (in *Alien*'s case especially) were not immediately understood. The choice of music for this Ridley Scott movie can be seen as a compromise, its final result being very different from Goldsmith's initial proposal. Luckily, Goldsmith's original score was recorded anyway and can be found on the most recent DVD releases, allowing us to compare whenever the director chose to replace a track with a pre-existing piece – many of which, ironically, came from Goldsmith's score for *Freud* (1962).

Planet of the Apes' strong suit lies first of all in its unusual and experimental orchestration; several parts of the movie are accompanied by serial music – as Goldsmith himself stated. The score's technique, however, might best be described as "free twelve-tone" rather than as seriality, as the latter would have required stricter schemes. We find no trace, therefore, of conventional themes, and the short rhythmic-timbric cells are the listener's only reference points. Some tracks of the score highlight an irregular and apparently "wild" rhythm (such as in THE HUNT). The *Alien* and *Outland* scores, written about a decade after *Planet of the Apes*, show a somewhat more ethereal and undetermined musical language which, despite the apparent calm, sharpens the sense of anxiety evoked by outer space. As remarked by Michel Chion,[110] *Alien*'s score appears closer to the style of Debussy, namely his first orchestral *Nocturne*, *Nuages*. This is due to the fact that the French composer's music, the language of which defies the central role of tonality, is considered among the foundations of the most cutting-edge musical thought of the 19th century. Although Debussy's music might not appear so hard to understand, its very lack of a clear and univocal tonal center hides an inner complexity. Tonal and harmonic uncertainty creates a sense of vagueness that perfectly applies to the representation of outer space. Goldsmith added his usual rhythmic energy to this harmonically-vague language in several parts of both movies; overall, though, his purpose was to highlight the characters' lack of certainty, rather than the movie's plot. Basically, though partially positive experiences may occur, space will always be incomprehensible and inaccessible to humanity, and that is why it is unrealistic to celebrate it with heroic *topoi* such as marches or fanfares.

Planet of the Apes, Goldsmith's second collaboration with director Franklin Schaffner after *The Stripper* (1963), was the start of an artistic union leading to the creation of some of the most significant pages in

---

[110] MICHEL CHION, *La musique au cinéma*, Paris, Fayard, 1998, p.238.

U.S. movie history, especially during the 1970s, with fairly well-known titles such as *Patton*, *Papillon* and *The Boys from Brazil*. Loosely based on a novel by Pierre Boulle, published in France in 1964, *Planet of the Apes* takes its characters and part of its plot from the eponymous book, using them to create quite a different story. The plot is simple: a group of astronauts, realizing their spaceship has broken down, manages to land on an apparently deserted planet. Soon they realize they have stumbled upon a very different era, as the year is 3900 AD. The planet, they discover, is inhabited. There are humans, but they're dumb and wild; apes, on the other hand, have created a defined and structured social civilization. Only one of the spacemen, Taylor (Charlton Heston), manages to survive; after being captured by the apes, he slowly builds a trusting relationship with female ape-scientist Zira (Kim Hunter), who helps him escape and enter the so-called *forbidden zone*. Here, in a final plot twist, Taylor realizes he had been on Earth all along, but that human civilization has long been obliterated, possibly due to a nuclear holocaust (bringing to mind the constant Cold War fears from the movie's era). The ending, therefore, gives a retroactive meaning to the movie's didactic and pessimistic message. Goldsmith's score is dynamic and modern, discarding melodic themes in favor of highlighting short cells of sound. Timbre takes center stage, thanks to unusual wind instruments such as the *shofar*, or ram's horn. This instrument, from Jewish liturgical heritage, creates a sound similar to a cold moan and is mainly used in the score's wildest track, THE HUNT, which accompanies a human-hunting sequence. Equally peculiar are the score's percussions, while traditional instruments are often employed in an unusual way, as we have already mentioned in our chapter about orchestration. Much of the score's timbric value is given by percussions: piano, xylophone, vibraphone and *cuíka*, among others. The sound is strictly orchestral, devoid of electronics with the exception of the echoplex, used to create an echo to the strings' *pizzicato*.[111] The movie's longstanding success matched the success of its score, which became a bestseller despite its "abstractness". The film paved the way for four more sequels as well as

---

[111] In the DVD audio commentary, Goldsmith defines this procedure "tapedelay".

80

a TV show. Leonard Rosenman wrote the score for the second episode,[112] while Goldsmith returned for the third, *Escape from the Planet of the Apes* (1971; directed by Don Taylor); the latter's score is considerably lighter than Goldsmith's previous one, due to the fact that the first part of the movie plays on the confrontation between evolved apes Zira and Cornelius and Cold-War USA between the end of the '60s and the beginning of the '70s; the tragic ending, however, brings both composer and audience back to the atmospheres of the first installment. The fourth and fifth movies were predictably less successful, though they still had a certain value within the saga.[113] More disappointing was the outcome of its namesake TV series – on air from September to December, 1974 – which was cancelled after 14 episodes without reaching a real conclusion. *Planet of the Apes* is actually a science-fiction story only in appearance: as the final twist retroactively explains, the movie's theme is not really mankind's exploration of the unknown. The inversion of roles in the movie is perhaps a tad schematic – a group of apes (orangutans, chimps, gorillas) forming a strongly hierarchical society – and the reversed point of view is used as an excuse for the hero to start a rebellion with the help of the most enlightened among his enemies. The story's underlying message, however, is far from being purely entertaining, and seeks to highlight the consequences of man's hate towards his equals and his fear of facing what is different.

For this exact reason Goldsmith strives to express the main character's uncertainties, as he finds himself in a future that might actually be the past. The composer particularly emphasizes the hero's rebellion against a system that regards him as little more than an object; once more the main character tragically finds himself alone and helpless, as his own helpers soon fall back into line to avoid exposing themselves to

---

[112] The second movie, *Beneath the Planet of the Apes* (1969; directed by Ted Post) is strictly connected to the first and completes its succession of events, ending with the planet's repeated destruction.

[113] The last two episodes in the saga are *Conquest of the Planet of the Apes* (1972) and *Battle for the Planet of the Apes* (1973), both directed by Jack Lee Thompson. Their scores were respectively written by Tom Scott and – again – by Rosenman.

risks. From a musical point of view, the composer immediately makes his intentions clear in the movie's opening Main Title, where a central melodic theme is disregarded in favor of rarefied, brief instrumental interjections. One of the few recognizable themes is executed by the piccolo. In the beginning, the piano insistently exposes a grave E flat with an increasingly fast rhythm, followed by a bass slide whistle (a peculiar kind of whistle) glissando. The repetition after the piano is followed by several percussions, such as kettledrums, *angklung* and gong (played with a metal stick), together with cellos and basses. The piccolo motif is introduced by the violin pizzicato alone:

[*Planet of the Apes* (1968), *Main Titles*, main theme]

The score's division in brief instrumental interjections is one of its main features; another one is the unconventional emission of sound from certain wind instruments, as well as the use of several kinds of percussions. The track THE HUNT, accompanying the sequence when humans are hunted down by the ape army, is the movie's first dramatic moment. This track shows the use of an unusual wind instrument, the *shofar* – which Goldsmith calls ram's horn – an animal (ram) horn employed in Jewish liturgy. Here the horn is used out of its canonic context, with the practical aim of presenting a sharp, barbaric timbre by producing a melodic interval (fifth ascending and descending), simple but very effective in terms of creating tension, thanks to the percussive rhythm added by kettledrums and long drum.

[*Planet of the Apes* (1968), *The Hunt*]

The scene, barely more than five minutes long, occurs about half an hour into the movie and represents its first and most disconcerting dramatic twist. In the movie's audio commentary, Goldsmith describes this moment from a musical point of view:

> It's an amazing scene when we think of the endless car chases in movies today. In comparison to the nihilism and destruction typical of many modern films, there is this scene, turned in a brilliant way. Frank Schaffner al

ways inserted some kind of humor in his pictures, like the idea of these simians (at the end of the scene, *a/n*) who boast of their hunting trophies like humans: it is a strong statement. In the shot of the horse, as the creature turns and we see that is a simian, the music has this organic feel, got, actually, by a ram's horn actually played, capable of emitting only two notes, but very effective ones. The idea is that we are dealing with (...) an upside down world. (...) The parallels are shocking in many ways, see that humans are being hunted and those usually hunted are the predators, it's a shocking statement. (...) I always want to preserve a primitive feel in the music, but the style of the music is quite modern. (...) It's written in a serial style technique, the twelve-tone system, not in the normal diatonic harmony. In many ways it seems abstract, but is very steady and carefully structured. At the time there were few scores made with this language.[114]

Among the unusual percussion instruments employed in this scene, we find the *cuika* (or *cuica*), which is a single-skin friction drum used in Latin America, brought to Brazil by African slaves. Possibly originated from a variation of the African *lion's roar*, it is usually employed in jazz and dance ensembles. This oft-neglected instrument is very interesting when used in contemporary music, especially from a timbric point of view, as it allows us to reach a whole range of new sounds. According to the variations in its use, it can produce very different effects: grumbles, wails, snorts, roars and high-pitched shrieks. When the stick is shortly and dryly rubbed, the result is similar to the call of a cuckoo. It is hard to obtain great dynamic variations from this instrument.[115]

The *vibraslap*: initially created as a substitute for the *quijada* or donkey jaw, it is formed by a curved rod of elastic steel; its two ends are affixed to a wooden sphere and to a thin, trapeze-shaped open wooden box, similar to a small Latin-American bell, working as a resonator. Inside the box there is a metal bar, connected to the trapeze's shorter side, with ten loose, moving rivets. By placing a cupped hand before the opening we might reach a sound similar to muffled trumpets. While executing this muffling effect one must be careful not to touch the

---

[114] Transcrip. of the composer's commentary to the *Planet of the Apes* 2004 DVD special edition.
[115] GUIDO FACCHIN, *Le percussioni*, Turin, Edt, 2000², p.409-411.

opening, as this might affect the uniformity of sound. By moving the hand it is possible to reach an open/closed sound. The instrument's dynamic range goes from *f* to *ff*.[116]

The *shofar* (or *ram's horn*), as previously stated, is used to obtain a menacing, barbaric sound.[117] This aerophone's origin is sacred – its religious use is described in the Bible's Book of Numbers (XXIX,1). It is created from a horn of sheep or goat killed in a ritual, and the cavity in its mouthpiece usually forms an ellipsis with the main cavity inside the horn. Its acoustic behavior is unusual, as it often produces two sounds within a fifth's distance from one another, namely a harmonic 2 together with a lower falsetto. When producing two sounds with a small horn, it is natural to start with the lowest and then moving (if possible) to the following one, mentally referencing a consonant pause; this is what happens in various signals given in the synagogue.[118]

[Example of Shofar]

---

[116] *Ibid.*, p.304.

[117] The movie's apes also use it as a military call and as a signal during their hunt. It's an example of mediated level, one of the three levels in scoring as theorized by Sergio Miceli: an *internal* musical method (a melody, an instrument etc) becoming part of the *external* score. Miceli cites the *internal* music played by Father Gabriel (Jeremy Irons) in *The Mission* (1986), an oboe piece which later becomes part of Morricone's score. Another good example is given by Zbigniew Preisner in *Trois Couleurs: Bleu* (1993).

[118] ANTHONY BAINES, *Brass Instruments: Their History and Development*, London, Faber and Faber, 1976 (this quote was taken from the Italian edition: ANTHONY BAINES, *Gli ottoni*, Turin, Edt, 1991, p.37).

In 1976, Goldsmith tried his hand at yet another science-fiction score, this time for *Logan's Run*, directed by Michael Anderson. The movie is set in a "perfectly autonomous and efficient" State-city from a hyper-technological future, where people are ruled by a superior entity similar to George Orwell's Big Brother from *1984*. The law states that any individual must stop living after turning thirty, in order to maintain the city's well-oiled efficiency. One youth, however, revolts against this absurd series of limitations: Logan (Michael York), together with a fellow female citizen, manages to escape the city after a series of dangerous adventures. Once outside, Logan and the girl discover a living (though degraded) reality, where an old man (Peter Ustinov) welcomes them into the Resistance. The futuristic plot, completely absurd from a contemporary point of view, is nevertheless disturbing as it shows the dystopian possibility of a society transforming and thus limiting personal choice. The score mirrors the city's sterility and lack of passion by choosing an atonal and monotonous language, with the addition of electronic effects to convey the idea of an emotionally and physically aseptic environment. The two marking tracks of the score are THE MONUMENT, an eight-minute sort of *suite* setting the pace for the whole score – and the final END OF THE CITY, a kind of musical catharsis highlighting the moment when the two main characters discover the hope of a different life. These tracks are the most famous in the whole score, so much that the composer has allowed them to stand on their own during concerts.

In his short analysis of Goldsmith's science fiction scores, Gary Kester finds some similarities between some parts of the *Logan's Run* score and the symphonic repertoire. The opening track – THE DOME –, for example, gradually builds up to a crescendo reminiscent of Richard Strauss's famous *Also Sprach Zarathustra* op.30.[119] The implied tension, significantly expressed by Goldsmith through free atonalism, gives way

---

[119] GARY KESTER, *An Analysis of the Science Fiction and Fantasy Scores of Jerry Goldsmith*, in "Legend-A Goldsmith Society publication", Autumn 1991, p.29. Strauss' piece, as we know, outside of its original context rooted in Nietzsche's philosophy, became a symbol of science-fiction movie scoring after Stanley Kubrick used it for his *2001: A Space Odyssey*.

to traditional melody towards the end (in the previously mentioned final track END OF THE CITY) sustained by an ensemble of strings, harp and woodwinds, just as the surviving citizens, exiting the artificial air and light of their city, discover a non-synthetic world for the first time.[120]

A liberally atonal magma of sounds, closely matching the sensations and situations on screen, is interposed with more lyrical havens, knowingly orchestrated and contextualized to serve their purpose. This score has been ascribed to a less-abstract kind of science fiction, as the happy ending imposed by the script, as well as the director's final result, clash both with the literary precedents on similar topics (the aforementioned *1984*) and with common sense; to this effect, Goldsmith proved consistent in ending a "difficult" score, built in close cohesion with the movie's subject matter, with a piece conveying a sort of mystic catharsis. This was one of the reasons why the movie was criticized, and its final result questioned. Goldsmith, at times, expressed his disappointment at the way directors handled the final parts of his scores, giving them a personal musical interpretation that was much different from what he had intended: the same happened, as we have already seen, with the score for *Alien*, written three years after *Logan's Run.*

Ever since his first futuristic movies – connected to an imaginary future life on Earth or to the representation of parts of space that are unknown due to our civilization's lack of technology – Goldsmith had favored hard-to-approach scores characterized by an extremely bold musical language. The composer had first tried his hand at this genre is sci-fi thriller *Seconds* (1966; directed by John Frankenheimer), which, rather than having a futuristic setting, was centered on an unprecedented act: the movie imagines a future where it is possible to change one's face – disturbing as it may sound – by visiting a dedicated agency,[121] and the whole plot is predictably influenced by the main

---

[120]   *Ibid.*

[121]   A similar topic was at the base of another movie scored by Goldsmith, the previously mentioned *Total Recall*, which showed the main character visiting a "virtual" travel agency. Such themes had developed in post-WWII sci-fi literature, and were later adapted for the screen; movies like *Blade Runner* (1982), *Total Recall* (1990) and *Minority*

character's choice in this sense. This 1960s movie is all the more significant as it is one of the first experiments in mixing different genres, striving to break away from Hollywood's strict genre rules. Frankenheimer would later become one of Hollywood's most in-demand action directors, and his editing rhythm proved crucial in setting the story's pace. Goldsmith felt the need to create a score based more on timbre and rhythm than on melody, though this might have resulted in less clarity of theme exposition. This score marked one of the composer's first experiments in integrating an orchestra with electronics, though in this case the chosen ensemble was not particularly large. Shaky violins and electronic echoes build up the monumental "explosion" of a church organ, performing the movie's Main Title for the first time. High-pitched violins move almost elliptically on the constant throbbing of kettledrums, creating a perturbing, almost funeral march-like theme. The theme is mostly employed in the movie's first part, with a peculiar variation during the face-surgery sequence when Goldsmith made a brutal use of strings; he would later do the same in other works such as *Gremlins* and *Twilight Zone- The Movie*.[122] As it almost always happens, Goldsmith also inserted a more lyric, nostalgic, almost pastoral passage in another part of the movie: in this case, when the main character (played by Rock Hudson) starts missing his old life. The deeply melancholic theme was created through the use of harp and violin, followed by piano. The same theme later becomes more threatening as the movie approaches its surprise ending.

Goldsmith's work on *Star Trek* started when the composer had already had twenty years' worth of experience, honing his orchestral expertise in a Straussian sense – increased by more experimental instrumentation – and, as far as structure was concerned, in a pseudo-Wagnerian sense. This kind of musical conception is less subtle than an "abstract" approach, and yet just as complex in its realization, as proven by Wagner's opera cycle *Der Ring des Nibelungen*. Interconnected movie sequels have often been linked by musical ties, through the use

---

Report (2002) are actually all based on Philip K. Dick's novels and short stories.
[122]   KESTER, *cit.*, p.28.

of themes being changed and deformed according to the situation on the screen. A movie score built on recurring themes might seem like the most obvious and easiest to create: but for a composer like Goldsmith, whose studies focused on the most cutting-edge languages of 20th century music, the opposite has actually proven true.

Fantasy movies and the concepts they are based on are not really new, as they spring from a literary and musical genre already very popular in the 19th century – one only needs to think of the fantastic tales written by Théophile Gautier, Poe and Hoffmann, and, musically speaking, of Hector Berlioz's creations. Movies of this kind might be considered – in a very simplistic way – as the search for an escape from reality, projecting the audience in a different, Utopian world that is better than the one we live in.

Goldsmith was often summoned to work on such pictures, which were certainly in tune with his sensibility. Strictly speaking, the golden age of *fantasy* movies can be roughly be placed after the release of Spielberg's *Close Encounters of the Third Kind* (1977): after that, the more "serious" approach to science fiction culminating in 1977's *Star Wars* (directed by George Lucas) parted ways with a rather optimistic sub-genre, spanning from *Close Encounters* and *E.T.* (1982) – both scored by John Williams – to movies produced under Steven Spielberg's patronage; a veritable factory forming directors like Joe Dante and Robert Zemeckis, creators of this genre's masterpieces (*Gremlins* and *Explorers*, the former; the *Back to the Future* trilogy, the latter).

Goldsmith's first contact with this genre occurred with a manifesto of sorts, *Twilight Zone- The Movie* (1983), which Spielberg and Dante directed together with John Landis and George Miller. Inspired by the TV series of the same name, on air in the US between 1959 and 1964, the movie is a curious and not always homogenous mash-up of fantasy, thriller and horror, with some comedic elements thrown in for good measure – in this sense matching the TV series' signature mixture of various genres. Since then, Goldsmith's contribution to this kind of movies was largely due to his stable working relationship with Joe

Dante: the composer scored the two *Gremlins* episodes (1984, 1990), *Explorers* (1985), *Innerspace* (1987) and *Small Soldiers* (1998).

To the same genre we can ascribe Goldsmith's work on a "comic book" movie – a trend stemming from the two *Batman* episodes directed by Tim Burton: *The Shadow* (1994; directed by Russell Mulcahy), as other less aesthetically pleasing films, allowed the composer to display his orchestral abilities and experiment on mixing electronics with orchestral ensembles – though the latter always remained Goldsmith's medium of choice. His most impressive result in this genre, however, was the previously mentioned score for *Legend*, not a very successful movie in spite of its complexity and attention to detail: for this score, as he rarely did, Goldsmith used a choir and voices to create a "magical" sound *continuum* inspired by Ravel's ballet *Daphnis et Chloé* (1912) as well as by Celtic music.[123] More Goldsmith works from the '80s include *Supergirl* (1984; directed by Jeannot Szwarc) – a female version of Donner's *Superman* (1978) famously scored by John Williams. The *Supergirl* movie worked as a test-bed for the massive use of a great orchestra with a strong brass component, and was a rare example of a Goldsmith score inspired by Williams, in the footsteps of the *Star Wars* trilogy and, obviously, of *Superman*. In more recent years, the composer wrote music for *Powder* (1995; directed by Victor Salva), the account of a paranormal case recalling both *The Twilight Zone* and *The X-Files*; this time, Goldsmith evoked the movie's topic with a score that was very similar to the one he had written for *Legend* and – consequentially – to the aforementioned ballet by Ravel.

Film Noir

As well as being an in-demand composer for action movies, which required an asserting kind of rhythm, Goldsmith was often hired for movies permeated by constant tension, such as horrors. A movie like

---

[123] Traditional Irish music is also found elsewhere in Goldsmith's production, e.g. adventure-thriller movie *The Ghost and the Darkness* (1996), the main theme of which was inspired by a traditional Celtic song.

Alien, after all, is in itself a reflection on cinematic narration about horror and fear. On fewer (though remarkable) occasions, the composer was called to try his hand at so-called *noir* movies, as they were defined by French movie critics; a genre comprised of stories about private detectives, gangsters, corrupt police officers and the like. The main characters in these movies, the *heroes*, are never morally spotless, which makes them all the more complex and interesting. Remarkable examples of this genre were already starting to appear at the dawn of the *talkies*: *Scarface, Shame of a Nation* (1932; directed by Howard Hawks), as well as other Warner Bros-produced titles from the end of the 1930s. The 1940s were the epitome of the *noir* movie era:[124] *The Maltese Falcon* (1941; directed by John Huston and based on a Dashiell Hammett novel), *Double Indemnity* (1944; directed by Billy Wilder, and based on James Cain), *The Killers* (1946; directed by Robert Siodmak; based on a Hemingway short story), *Brute Force* (1947) and *The Naked City* (1948), both directed by Jules Dassin; the trend continued into the 1950s with *The Asphalt Jungle* (1950; directed by John Huston), *While the City Sleeps* (1956; directed by Fritz Lang) and the masterpiece *Touch of Evil* (1958; directed by Orson Welles and scored by Henry Mancini).[125] *Noirs* are hard to define, as they move away from traditional detective stories by presenting vaguer descriptions of characters and settings. In the best examples of the genre, even the characters who should represent justice, the "healthy" and morally noble side of the story, belong to a world marked by a moral ambiguity and by a sense of loss, disenchantment and impending death. The literary vein of this genre is wide, spanning from the most distinguished examples of Raymond Chandler, Dashiell Hammett and James Cain to contemporary novelist James Ellroy, not to mention a series of minor writers – Jim Thompson, Lionel

---

[124] 1941 is usually marked as start of the "main" *noir* age, with John Huston's *The Maltese Falcon*, while its end is marked in 1958 by Orson Welles' *Touch of Evil*.

[125] Many of these movies were scored by Miklós Rózsa, who became an emblematic composer of this genre before incarnating, a few years later, the historical-religious one. Henry Mancini, on the other hand, wrote an Afro-Cuban score for the aforementioned Orson Welles movie, where the main character, unorthodox cop Hank Quinlan, was played by the director himself.

White, Cornell Woolrich, among others – who provided almost every plot for the best cinematic adaptations. The most emblematic characters are the private eye and the dark lady, and their shifty relationship is one of the *topoi* of this genre. The anti-hero, a gangster or other powerful figure oppressing a community, is usually connected to the female lead, as well as being the object of an investigation which is typically opposed by the corrupt, official police force. The settings are urban, populated by characters with little to no morals. There is a wide sense of disenchantment. The noir movie tradition became lost in the following decades, giving the genre an aura of exceptionality. A new wave of the genre, inspired by the seminal originals, was created in the 1970s: among its most remarkable examples we find *The Long Goodbye* (1973; directed by Robert Altman), as well as other adaptations from Raymond Chandler, one of the most emblematic *noir* writers in history. The most important movie of this age, however, is Roman Polanski's *Chinatown* (1974), scored by Goldsmith himself. The composer was hired to write this score after a series of less remarkable pictures such as the little-known *The Crimebuster* (1962; directed by Boris Sagal) and *The Detective* (1968; directed by Gordon Douglas and centered on private eye Tony Rome, played by Frank Sinatra, who also starred in two more sequels). Another one of Goldsmith's experiences in this genre was *The Last Run* (1971; started by John Huston and completed by Richard Fleischer), a sort of "on the road" *noir* story. A former gangster, – played by George C. Scott – who has retired to Portugal after a life of crime in Chicago, is hired to escort an escaped convict to France. The main character, a disenchanted loser, sacrifices his life when he discovers he still has something to believe in, namely the love he feels for the convict's woman. While *The Last Run* can be considered an atypical *noir*, *Chinatown* is closer to the genre's conventions, though its choices in direction and script are anything but obvious. Written by Robert Towne and directed by Roman Polanski, this movie recalls the best examples of the genre from the 1930s and '40s. By recreating *noir* settings and ploys – the movie is set in 1930s Los Angeles – Towne delivered a strong final result, emphasized by Polanski and by a gifted cast of characters: Jack Nicholson, Faye Dunaway and director John Huston, the latter starring in a supporting role. Both here and in *L.A. Confidential* (1997), a subsequent, remarkable example of this genre, set in the 1950s – the orchestral score is interspersed with period songs, usually jazz standards – in order to create a sort of setting identification through the use of popular music. In both cases, incidental music written from scratch is reduced to few – though forceful – pieces for a total of little more than half an hour out of about two hours of movie. This makes it an essential presence focused exclusively on specific moments. Although Goldsmith's score for this Polanski movie is considered one of his most successful and true-to-genre works, the composer did not have much time to write it, as he started working when the movie's editing had already been completed and post-production was well on its way. Goldsmith was chosen to replace a previous composer, Philip Lambro, whose work had been rejected by Paramount. Even before writing even a single note, merely by watching the edited movie, the composer understood that, in that particular case, he had to base his work on timbre, rather than on musical themes. First of all, therefore, he realized he needed a specific sound blend, of a chamber music nature, and selected four pianos, four harps, percussions, a solo trumpet and strings. Goldsmith recalls how part of his creative process developed in close relation to the chosen ensemble:

> I don't know where the hell I came up with that, but I thought immediately of that combination. I had no actual music to go along with it, though, at the stage. I don't believe in all this talk about orchestration – it's really quite subservient to what the *music* is, the actual notes. Anyone with any kind of technique can make an orchestra sound marvelous for two hours even without any musical content.[126]

With the help of orchestrator Arthur Morton, and by using the small ensemble he had conceived, Goldsmith wrote a score that, though not built around a theme, was closely connected to the movie's atmo-

---

[126] MORGAN, *Knowing the Score*, op.cit., p.178.

sphere. The only recognizable musical theme is the memorable and melancholy LOVE THEME FROM CHINATOWN, for solo trumpet and small ensemble. The theme has the same function (a sort of "stalking horse") as the liaison between private eye J.J. Gittes (Nicholson) and Evelyn Mulwray (Dunaway): the nostalgic and evocative melody is actually completely misleading, as the true driving force in the plot is the character of Noah Cross (Huston), a powerful and corrupt businessman who is also Evelyn's father. The final triumph of the domineering Cross, both in private (his incestuous relationship with his daughter, which is not discovered until it is too late) and in public (the bribery of LA's water supply on which Gittes is investigating) is the climax of a dark story offering no possible release. Noah Cross only appeared in a handful of scenes, but Goldsmith immediately realized his dramatic importance and, from a musical point of view, provided him with a musical device by associating him to the timbre of a scratchy Latin-American percussion instrument, the güiro, originally hailing from Africa. In different parts of Latin America the güiro , apparently named after a piece of fruit, is also known as "samba cucumber", carracho, guitcharo, calabazo, carrasca or rallador (grater), guayo and gracé. I.Stravinskij was the first to include it in an orchestra (*Le sacre du printemps*, 1913), followed by D.Milhaud (*Le boeuf sur le toit*, 1920), M.Ravel (*L'enfant et les sortilèges*, 1920/1925), A.Roldán (*Rítmicas* nn.5 e 6, 1930) and E.Varèse (*Ionisation*, 1933).[127]

Chinatown, therefore, is a very forceful example of a dramatically significant use of timbre – produced by a peculiar small ensemble and by a scratchy instrument – which manages to overshadow the (albeit well-known) solo trumpet theme. Several years elapsed before Goldsmith had the chance to try his hand at this genre again. In 1992 he was offered the score for *The Public Eye* (directed by Howard Franklin), a fairly decent Universal movie, starring Joe Pesci as a crime news photographer getting into trouble over his platonic love for a nightclub owner, a young widow played by Barbara Hershey. In this case, however, Goldsmith's music – already written and recorded for the movie – was

---

[127] GUIDO FACCHIN, *Le percussioni, op.cit.*, p.264-265.

rejected and replaced with a score by Mark Isham, a younger jazz trumpeter and composer. According to Mike Ross-Trevor,[128] one of the best sound engineers in movie scoring, Goldsmith's music was perfectly worthy of being used, just like many of his other rejected scores, some of which were even better then the selected ones. Ross-Trevor is one of the few people who had the chance to hear this particular work: unlike other scores rejected by production studios, the music for *The Public Eye* was never commercialized on its own. Five years after this controversial experience, Goldsmith accepted a somewhat similar assignment, though with a very different approach: composing the score for *L.A. Confidential* (1997; directed by Curtis Hanson). Both the picture and its music recall the atmospheres from *Chinatown*, though *L.A. Confidential* has a stronger and more explicit violent component. The movie, partly based on a novel by James Ellroy and steeped in period music, mixes tragedy and violence with a few elements of comedy and troubled love, depicted in a somewhat stylized way. The movie's best sequences are also the most violent, both in editing and in direction: the scuffle at the police station, accompanied by the track BLOODY CHRISTMAS,[129] and the final showdown at the Victory Motel, underlined by tracks SHOOTOUT[130] and THE GOOD LAD.[131] The story revolves around three Los Angeles police agents dealing with crime and corruption: Jack Vincennes (played by Kevin Spacey), who is more interested in the comfortable life provided by his contribution to a TV series; Edmund Exley (Guy Pierce), an idealistic and ambitious youth; Bud White (Russell Crowe), a heavy-handed but uncompromising agent. The historical setting is 1950s Los Angeles, where organized crime is devoid of a central power after the fall of Mickey Cohen. The main plot explores a few of the main characters' personal issues, such as White's love for high-end call girl Lynn Bracken (Kim Basinger), who works for rich Pierce

---

[128]   Mike Ross-Trevor, as told to DIRK WICKENDEN, *Home Is Where the Heart Is: a Conversation with Mike Ross-Trevor*, in "Soundtrack!", vol.19, no.74, Summer 2000, p.42.

[129]   Cd Varèse Sarabande Vsd-5885, track#1 (first half).

[130]   *Ibid.*, track#9.

[131]   *Ibid.*, track#10.

Patchett (David Strathairn), a "businessman" linked to shady characters. Patchett's "business" specializes in prostitutes who are look-alikes
of famous actresses – Lynn herself being modeled on Veronica Lake.
Exley, on the other hand, works as a cop in the hope of catching his
father's murderer, an unknown policeman he calls by the name of
'Rollo Tomasi': his eventual discovery, however, will be a bitter surprise. Vincennes spends his days giving hunches to his friend Sid
Hudgens (Danny De Vito), the editor of a gossip rag, and working as a
consultant for a TV series called *Badge of Honor*. The police station is run
by Captain Dudley Smith (James Cromwell) who later proves to be as
corrupt as all the other members of the police and the law. At the beginning of the movie, agent Dick Stensland causes a few Mexican pris-
oners to be beaten up at the police station: this opens a Pandora's box
of corruption and murder, including the death of Stensland himself
and of his lover Susan Lefferts, another one of Patchett's call girls. In
spite of their personal differences, White and Exley join forces to expose the authority figures tied up in the crimes. Goldsmith based his
score on a few recurring themes: the trumpet – recalling the atmospheres Bernstein had evoked in *On the Waterfront* as well as Goldsmith's own *Chinatown* score – which appears in its most complete
form on the track THE VICTOR;[132] a love theme[133] underlining the liaison
between Bud White and Lynn Bracken; the *Rollo Tomasi theme*, a figuration connected to this mysterious character.[134] Action sequences, on
the other hand, are underlined by self-sufficient pieces. The "final
showdown" is a typical Goldsmith finale, similar to the longer one he
would create a few years later for *Hollow Man*. Other, minor works of
Goldsmith's in this genre are *Shamus* (1972; directed by Buzz Kulik) and
The Don Is Dead (1973; directed by Richard Fleischer).

---

[132] The sequence can be seen in chapters 40 and 41 of the commercialized DVD version
(*see*.bibliography/videography); the core piece is track#11 of the soundtrack CD.

[133] DVD, chapter 20. CD: tracks #1 (part 2) and #4 (part 2) in a different form.

[134] Exley explains this fact in chapter 25 of the DVD. The theme can be heard after
Vincennes' murder, in chapter 30; this theme never appears on the CD, although
there is a track by the same name.

Action, thriller, war

Goldsmith's composing activity was a constant series of exercises on the concept of rhythm, a musical parameter he was fond of highlighting above all others. His orchestras, in particular, thrived on the frenetic rhythm of action sequences often found in "restless" movie genres such as thriller, action and war.

When working on war movies, Goldsmith usually restrained from adopting conventional formulas, choosing instead to highlight a contradiction to the images on the screen. Hence his choice of an elegiac tone for *Patton*, to name just one, with the result of focusing on the personality of a man rather than the one of a victorious but misunderstood leader. Action movies, on the other hand, being overall more "cookie cutter", allowed him to write a few above-average pieces, though his composing effort was often wasted on low-grade productions; that is why we find many similar pieces in different action movies, and why they are often more significant in terms of technique than of inspiration or language. A few remarkable moments can nevertheless be noticed, such as in the previously mentioned score for *Total Recall*. A high point in action movie scoring, Goldsmith's work on this film later influenced other similar scores, though not necessarily written for science-fiction. The result is even more relevant given that the movie itself is a genre hybrid – on the one hand it is pure action, with chasing sequences, plot twists and misunderstandings; on the other, it is a reflection on the future based on a short story by Philip K.Dick. Having previously worked on more "difficult" science fiction movies, Goldsmith was able to produce consistently memorable results. A brief description of this work highlights the importance of the orchestra and of its catchy rhythm:

> The score for Verhoeven's *Total Recall* spits out boiling lava from each bar, being pushed by a dizzying internal violence, which we may recognize both in its rhythmic choice and in its impressive, almost apocalyptic

"firepower" of sound. The driving force of the whole score can be identi-
fied at the beginning of THE DREAM: a typical "limping" and irregular Goldsmith march serving as a base for a linear and airy brass theme, supported by other, strictly electronic rhythmic effects. It is peculiar, in this respect, to notice how Goldsmith used electronics as an orchestral component, instead of giving them a privileged role (this is especially noticeable
in THE HOLOGRAM, where the sound level reaches an almost insufferable
pitch): equally important is the heavy, radical atonality of the score, interspersed with dreamy sounds and "astral" modulations sometimes opposed to a countermelody played by a cello and followed by the whole
string section.[135]

All through the '90s, after the success of *Total Recall*, the composer was
commissioned several other action-movie scores, more or less connected to a pseudo-scientific genre, such as *Chain Reaction* (1996; directed
by Andrew Davis). A less "evolved" kind of action, with fewer existential implications about the future of mankind and the planet, can be
found in more conventional movies such as *Executive Decision* (1996;
directed by Stuart Baird), *Air Force One* (1997; directed by Wolfgang
Petersen), and *U.S. Marshals* (1998; directed by Stuart Baird). These
scores, rather insignificant from an expressive point of view, are nonetheless remarkable for Goldsmith's technical care and expertise. The
Executive Decision score, for example, being more than an hour and a
half long and including different versions of the same tracks, is a sure
sign of the composer's never-ending search for the best possible result,
perhaps worthy of a better cause. Out of this group of movies from the
second half of the '90s, *Air Force One* is the most "noble" example. The
cinematic result is almost poor, though Goldsmith makes the most of it
showing a different approach to an action plot that, though not exactly
trite, is nonetheless rather formulaic:

> With *Air Force One*, Goldsmith creates sort of musical blueprint for action
> movies. The very triumphant, Strauss-like main theme has the threaten-
> ing solemnity of an *epicedium*, whereas in the wildest pages the com-

---

[135]   ROBERTO PUGLIESE, *Atto di forza*, in "Segnocinema", no.46, November/December 1990, p.78.

poser's diabolic counterpoint and instrumental ability stand out over any possible comparison (THE HIJACKING). There is a prevalence of the typical syncopated rhythms from Goldsmith's most pressing moments (...), such as the use of a piano as a percussion instrument and the overwhelming mellowness of strings.[136]

For thrillers, Goldsmith composed scores mixing action with elegy such as the one for *Sleeping with the Enemy* (1991; directed by Joseph Ruben), a conventional star vehicle for Julia Roberts ending with the annihilation of the movie's main source of distress (in this case, a violent and psychotic husband reminiscent of Adrian Lyne's 1987 *Fatal Attraction*); while the movie clearly wants the audience to sympathize with the female lead,[137] it still manages to cast a more ambiguous and problematic light on the simple starting motive naively describing the couple's apparent happiness.

> Do not be fooled by the relaxing and elegiac opening theme MORNING ON THE BEACH: we are dealing with a deeply disturbing and threatening score, though not as violent and aggressive as other works by Goldsmith. In the following THE FUNERAL we may already notice a pressing polytonal interpretation of the same theme, fragmented and rhythmic; and as the tension grows, the music also moves towards the thrilling peaks of percussive and syncopated agitation (THE RING) that are typical of this American composer. The main theme, in any case, is repeatedly quoted and transformed (THE STORM) becoming distorted or extremely dramatic, such as in the wonderful THE CARNIVAL.[138]

Other, more "classic" thrillers – after the turning point of *Basic Instinct* – are *Malice* (1993; directed by Harold Becker) and *The Vanishing* (1993; directed by George Sluizer; a remake of a Dutch movie, from a few

---

[136] ROBERTO PUGLIESE, *Air Force One*, in "Segnocinema", no.88, November/December 1998, p.79.
[137] Goldsmith abstains from intervening in a sequence where, while having intercourse with his wife, the husband plays a CD of Berlioz's *Symphonie Fantastique* booming out the *Dies Irae* section from the last movement, *Songe d'une nuit de Sabba*: such details, among others, showcase the drastic approach of certain Hollywood scripts, especially towards this kind of movies.
[138] ROBERTO PUGLIESE, *A letto con il nemico*, in "Segnocinema", no.51, September/October 1991, p.87.

years before, by the same director).

The war films that Goldsmith participated in during the '60s and '70s stem from the American and foreign movies appearing on the cinematic scene in the decade after WWII. Such pictures, especially those dating back from the composer's beginnings, were often patriotic, as the era of "anti-war" movies was yet to come. During the'60s and '70s, moreover, as the U.S. was deep in the Vietnam war quagmire, the public needed to see a "positive" interpretation of past conflicts: this led to the creation of some openly rhetoric and nationalistic movies such as *The Green Berets* (1968; by John Wayne and Ray Kellog); though it may seem otherwise, even a movie like *MacArthur* (1977; directed by Joseph Sargent), on which Goldsmith himself worked, is actually quite reactionary. Still, from this particular score, we must at least save the MACARTHUR MARCH, often performed by the composer and forming, together with the main theme from *Patton* (1970), the so-called *The Generals Suite*, recorded and performed several times by the author himself. When examining the composer's choices, moreover, we must not forget the importance of a financial and productive component: such movies, whether blandly or openly propagandistic, were often important productions representing good career opportunities. Goldsmith's first war movie was an obscure British documentary from 1961, *General with the Cockeyed Id* – on which we have little information, though the score might still be found on bootleg recordings. His first official contact with the genre was in 1963, with *A Gathering of Eagles* (directed by Delbert Mann) which, rather than a war movie *per se*, was a drama set in a military base, of revolving around an officer's wife and her difficulty in adapting to military life.

After these two occasions , the composer's work on this genre became much more intense: in just two years, from 1965 to 1966, he worked on no less than five war movies. *Von Ryan's Express* (1965; directed by Mark Robson; starring Frank Sinatra); *Morituri* (1965; directed by Bernhard Wicki; starring Marlon Brando); *In Harm's Way* (1965; directed by Otto Preminger; starring John Wayne and Kirk Douglas); *The Blue Max* (1966; directed by John Guillermin; perhaps Goldsmith's most successful "war" score) and *The Sand Pebbles* (1966; directed by Robert Wise). During those two years the composer also worked on a melodrama, two comedies, a western and a thriller, as well as keeping his TV commitments (*Voyage to the Bottom of the Sea*, *Gunsmoke*, *The Loner*, *The Legend of Jesse James*, *Jericho*): it was a period of intense activity that saw him diving headfirst into war and western, two of the most typical movie genres in America.

Goldsmith's score for *The Sand Pebbles* earned him his third Oscar nomination, after *Freud* and *A Patch of Blue*; set in the Far East during the 1920s, the movie stars Steve McQueen as an American sailor involved in an exotic war adventure: hence the intense pages of the score, making ample use of music to characterize the Chinese setting. Such *local color* can also be found in other scores, especially those for movies set in the Far East, like *High Velocity* (1974; directed by Remi Kramer) and *Inchon* (1981; directed by Terence Young) or in Africa, like *Congo* (1995; directed by Frank Marshall and based on a Michael Crichton novel) and *The Ghost and the Darkness* (1996; directed by Stephen Hopkins; starring Michael Douglas). Later on, Goldsmith's commitments on war-action movies became further and further apart: the last great example was *Patton* (1970; directed by Franklin J. Schaffner), for which the composer chose an elegiac and intimate approach rather than a "fierce" one; it is noteworthy how the music written for this long-winded movie is very spare and focused on limited sequences, like the two remarkable PATTON MARCH and WINTER MARCH (also known as GERMAN MARCH). The main character's military march theme is noticeable for its use of a trumpet sound "doubled" by the *echoplex*, creating the impression of two trumpets playing from a distance. More conventional in its contraposition of the Americans and the Japanese is the music for *Tora!Tora!Tora!* (1970; directed by Richard Fleischer), showing some similarities to Goldsmith's 1966 score for *The Blue Max*. Out of the three *Rambo* movies which Goldsmith scored in the '80s (1982, 1985, 1988), centered on the famous character played by Sylvester Stallone, , the second and third episode can be regarded as more distinctly "war-like" – the composer's music, however, was less pompous than it might be expected.[139] Broadly speaking, *Under Fire* (1983; directed by Roger Spottiswoode), set in Nicaragua during the Sandinista revolution, can also be considered a war movie; in this score, just like in *Patton*, Goldsmith chose to highlight the doleful point of view of the main character – a war photographer played by Nick Nolte – rather than gloating in the guerrilla element of the story. From a timbric point of view, the composer employed Caribbean percussions to give the music a Latin tone, and wrote many of the pieces for guitar and orchestra, having Pat Metheny at his disposal as a solo performer. More recently, after a lapse of several years, Goldsmith went back to a "war score", albeit an ironic one, with *Small Soldiers* (1998; directed by Joe Dante). This score was self-referencing on two levels – in relation to previous war movies such as *Patton* and *Rambo*, and to Goldsmith's longtime collaboration with Dante, himself a lover of crossing genres and *pastiches*. It is remarkable how:

> The main theme (ASSEMBLY LINE) is so pompously martial as to become a caricature: the many following citations (from *Gremlins* to *Rambo* to *Patton*, and we even catch a glimpse of Morricone's *For a Few Dollars More*), together with military and patriotic pieces, clearly define the score as a fearless exercise in style: fanfares, drums, guitars and pipes evoke war (ROLL CALL), but the sudden appearance of bassoons, woodwinds and harps (PREPARE FOR ASSAULT) "winks" at the audience suggesting a joke, while the score's overall structure is powerfully majestic (the brass in TRUST ME) and shows a dazzling orchestral color.[140]

Musical amusement aside, here's how Pugliese comments the composer's work, highlighting its eclecticism:

> It becomes apparent, in short, that no matter his field of work, Goldsmith is now an all-around composer with virtually infinite resources.[141]

---

[139] A fourth episode in the *Rambo* series (*John Rambo*, 2008), shot after Goldsmith's death and scored by Brian Tyler, paid homage to the original composer by using the 1982 movie's main theme.

[140] ROBERTO PUGLIESE, *Small Soldiers*, in "Segnocinema", no.95, January/February 1999, p.78. The tracks' titles match the record published by Varèse Sarabande.

[141] *Ibid.*

Horror

The forerunners of the two main horror cycles in Goldsmith's career (*The Omen* and *Poltergeist*) are a mere handful of titles: *The Mephisto Waltz* (1971; directed by Paul Wendkos; the score is centered on the *dies irae* theme and on the use of avant-garde timbric motifs, especially in strings); and *The Other* (1972; directed by Robert Mulligan), for which the composer approached, as he had rarely done before or since, 20th century levels of experimentation connected to cutting-edge atonalism and aleatoric music, not only in certain sequences but in the score as a whole.

We have already discussed Goldsmith's work on *The Omen*, especially in relation to the relationship between composer and director; Goldsmith's other remarkable contribution to this genre is represented by the *Poltergeist* movies. The *Poltergeist* cycle is formed by three movies – as well as a TV show starting in the mid-'90s; Goldsmith scored the first two installments in the series: *Poltergeist* (1982; directed by Tobe Hooper) and *Poltergeist II- The Other Side* (1986; directed by Brian Gibson). The two scores have several points in common, as they are split between the sweet and lulling CAROL ANNE THEME – connected to the young, ESP-gifted main character and originating a never-ending series of distortions – and the use of expressionism, reminiscent of Alban Berg's work, in the most violent tracks like TWISTED ABDUCTION and NIGHT OF THE BEAST. The *Poltergeist* score is remarkable for the sheer length of its musical sequences which, at first listen, may even be regarded as symphonic poems. Besides the aforementioned TWISTED ABDUCTION, we might recall ESCAPE FROM SUBURBIA and NIGHT VISITOR/NO COMPLAINTS, both between seven and nine minutes long; two of the tracks, IT KNOWS WHAT SCARES YOU and REBIRTH, are just one long piece from the same sequence (the "rebirth scene"), split in two parts for a total of sixteen minutes. *Poltergeist*, more than other movies, uses music as an integral part of its final effect. Written and produced by Steven Spielberg, the movie is proof of one of the rare, albeit significant, collaborations between the director and Goldsmith – so much so that, during one interview, the composer stated that his post-production reference was not the movie's official director, Tobe Hooper, but Spielberg himself. This (unfortunately limited) professional relationship continued the following year with *Twilight Zone - The Movie*, a collective work created in celebration of the famous 1960s TV show, and in 1984 as Spielberg produced Joe Dante's *Gremlins*. A strictly symphonic score with no electronic element, the music for *Poltergeist* was created by mixing different musical styles while following the plot's dramatic development – besides Carol Anne's theme, which in its original version is basically a lullaby (sung by a white voice chorus in the finale), the other motifs are atonal or impressionistic: the score, therefore, can almost be considered a paradigm of the composer's body of work and of his complex approach to movie scoring. Carol Anne's theme, no doubt the most immediate and recognizable of the score, appears in its complete form – a simple ABA – at the beginning and the end of the movie, while during the course of the plot it can only be heard in fragments. Among the movie's secondary themes we find the 'theme of light' (from track THE LIGHT) emerging when the character of Dr Lesh explains the nature of the "light" leading to another dimension:[142] this motif is significantly modified in CONTACTING THE OTHER SIDE and again in REBIRTH; there's also a "jagged" theme representing the phantom intruders, a remarkable version of which can be heard in the track NIGHT VISITOR. Other tracks, more impressionistic and descriptive in nature, are used to musically "paint" the knotty tree in the Freeling family garden and to denote, through the use of grim sounds, the figure of the Beast in the movie's most intense sequences. Some scenes present a stylistic similarity to the *Alien* score, especially the use of brass for the musical description of the Beast – comparable to a similar method employed for the alien in Scott's movie – and to the Cloud sequence in *Star Trek: The Motion Picture*, in the use of long woodwind and string arpeggios. In such a rich score – about 70 minutes of music for a 110 minutes long movie – music is essential to the final result in two sequences especially: the six minutes long abduction scene (track TWISTED ABDUCTION) and the over 15 minutes of the "rebirth scene" (tracks IT KNOWS WHAT SCARES YOU and REBIRTH).[143]

---

[142] The scene can be enjoyed in chapter 25 of the commercialized DVD.
[143] Abduction scene: chapters 15-17 on the DVD edition; rebirth scene: chapters 31-35.

Adventure and exoticism

The success of Goldsmith's work and the many offers he received for epic and adventure movies, almost invariably set in places Hollywood considered "exotic", such as Africa or the Middle and Far East, might have clashed with the composer's musical education and personal taste, which was based on a never-ending study of harmony and timbre; at first listen, in fact, Goldsmith's scores for the previously mentioned sci-fi (*Planet of the Apes*, *Alien*, *Outland*) and horror movies (*The Mephisto Waltz*, *The Other*) are very different from the ones we shall examine in this section. Background aside, we might say that Goldsmith was born to write epic music, rich in instrumental inventions and especially remarkable for its rhythm and dizzying orchestral course. Even more so than John Williams, who competed with him for the best-paid commissions of the '70s and '80s – before other, younger composers such as Poledouris, Horner and Zimmer appeared on the scene to surpass their record. Goldsmith managed to overcome Williams in the kind of movies described in this chapter, while his colleague took the lead – just barely – in science-fiction and fantasy movies, for no other reason than because his music was more approachable. Although Goldsmith could not give free rein to his musical research while working on these movies, he could at least use their – often disheartening – lack of drama (this was especially true of thrillers and action films) to exercise his orchestral expertise, with the help of his trusty aides Arthur Morton and Alexander Courage. This genre in particular shows an unabashed use of stereotypes about geographical locations, of which the Hollywood industry maintains an almost romantic vision – considering them exotic just for being far from the Western world. Almost every movie in this genre has a token indigenous villain, – Arabic, Chinese or Far-Eastern – or even an intentionally comical Russian, the number one public enemy from the Cold War era. Goldsmith often approached these scores by integrating his orchestra with *ethnic* elements, though he never presumed to illustrate the movie's setting in a philological way; local color was usually provided, however, by certain percussions or wind instruments. Goldsmith's blueprint score for adventure-exotic movies, *The Wind and the Lion* (1975; directed by John Milius), is in great part emblematic for it use of an almost band-like instrumentation. "Moroccan" percussions are prevailing both in a rhythmic and in an environmental sense, being the driving force of almost the whole production; the score's texture, composed by simple and effective themes, is made epic by the use of brass instruments. Consider the B flat trumpet soaring, in the Main Title, after the percussive introduction and the initial appearance of horns; the piece starts with a "limping" rhythm created by percussions, similar to other of Goldsmith's "uneven" musical pieces. Such syncopated scanning can be found in several of his scores – the most poignant appearing in science fiction movies such as *Capricorn One* (1978) and *Total Recall*, where the opening titles start with an uncertain, though pressing, marching rhythm.

For adventure movies set in exotic locations, such as *The Wind and the Lion*, the composer used rhythm and timbre to give the audience an immediate idea of the environment and to convey a sense of impending danger. Both adventure and war are found in the previously mentioned score for *The Sand Pebbles* (1966), which mixes the rhythmic energy of its action sequences with moments of schematic Chinese exoticism, provided by characterizing pentatonic melodies. Between these two last pictures, in the years going from 1966 to 1975, Goldsmith did not work on traditional adventure movies – concentrating his effort on westerns, war movies and on his first sci-fi (*Planet of the Apes*) and horror experiments. He nonetheless managed to reach a spare but effective result with the biopic *Papillon* (1973; directed by Franklin J. Schaffner; screenplay by Dalton Trumbo and Lorenzo Semple jr), a score revolving around a typically French waltz theme connected to the origins of Henri Charrière, the real-life Papillon. The great Papillon character, played by Steve McQueen, balances out even the movie's excessive length, which takes away some of the freedom of spirit the story was supposed to symbolize. Just like *Patton* – another one of Goldsmith's collaborations with Schaffner – this score is comprised of barely over forty minutes of music for a two and a half hour long movie. After 1975, thanks to the success of *The Wind and the Lion* – proven by the score's frequent performances in concert suites, – Goldsmith's adventure movie work became more and more intense. Some of his exotic-adventurous scores from this time include: *The First Great Train Robbery* (1978; directed by Michael Crichton and set in 19th century Great Britain; its remarkable and vivacious *overture* was successfully performed live as well); *Masada: the Heroic Fortress* (1981; directed by Boris Sagal; a TV mini-series set during Roman occupation in Palestine and based on the famous *Judean War* by Flavius Josephus; a score in which rhythm, epic, orchestral and melodic virtuosism reach their fullest result – perhaps one of the best works of Goldsmith's career); *The Challenge* (1982; directed by John Frankenheimer and set in Japan); *Baby – The Secret of the Lost Legend* (1985; directed by Bill W.L. Norton and set in central Africa); *King Solomon's Mines* (1985; directed by Jack Lee Thompson; also set in central Africa, this score shows some rather difficult (albeit somewhat shallow) passages for orchestra, as well as thinly disguised citations of Wagner's *Valkyrie Ride*); and central Africa again, ten years later, for *Congo* (directed by Frank Marshall). *Lionheart* (1987; directed by Franklin J. Schaffner and set during the Crusades, is one of the best examples of a Goldsmith score tinged with simple but effective epic elements; it was also his first work to be released almost integrally – about one hour and twenty minutes of music – and directly, with an official two-disc edition published by Varèse Sarabande). The second and third episode in the series centered on angry ex-marine John Rambo – *Rambo - First Blood Part 2* (1985; directed by George Pan Cosmatos), set in Vietnam, and *Rambo 3* (1988; directed by Peter MacDonald), set in Afghanistan – despite their obvious connection to the war genre, can also be considered exotic. An airy and light score, though with a few of Goldsmith's trademark moments of tension, was written for *Medicine Man* (1991), a pseudo-environmentalist story set in the Amazon rainforest for which the composer created a fairly unassuming backdrop. *The River Wild* (1994; directed by Curtis Hanson), is a thriller almost exclusively set on a boat sailing over the Colorado rapids. *First Knight,* Hollywood's rehashing of the Arthurian legend, is an hour and a half of high-level instrumental music for a second-rate movie and perhaps Goldsmith's best work for an epic-adventurous story:

> Swamped as we are by the current medieval movies and scores, almost taking us back to the 1950s and the picaresque Metro age of Rózsa, Jerry Goldsmith stands out for his unmistakably modern and aggressive approach. Far from reaching for "ancient sounds", Goldsmith prefers to recall his own epic style from the '70s and '80s (...): the orchestra is out in full force, especially the brass section (ARTHUR'S FANFARE) and the horns, required to perform high virtuosisms with rapidly ascending and descending outlines. The Camelot theme (which becomes, in a broader sense, Guinevere's love theme) is achingly lyrical and expertly constructed, the battle scenes (RAID ON LEONESSE is a mini-essay on orchestration which we owe to Goldsmith's most faithful aide, Alexander Courage), where the composer widely adopts his own syncopated and limping rhythmic imprimatur, are extraordinary; the use of choir (ARTHUR'S FAREWELL) is pressing and archaic.[144]

The Ghost and the Darkness (1996), a thriller set in Africa, mixes with surprising ease an Irish component with the main African rhythm and percussions; in this score, more than in others, the use of brass and French horns is obvious and imposing: for example in the THEME FROM THE GHOST AND THE DARKNESS, where horns expose the main theme after the wind instruments have introduced the "Irish" figuration. In 1997 Goldsmith worked on mountain adventure *The Edge* (directed by Lee Tamahori), managing to create a more ambitious main theme, almost in the footsteps of Vaughan-Williams' and Elgar's British tradition:

> Since the enunciation of its dramatic main theme (LOST IN THE WILD), this score appears more melodic than ever. Quick and heated action moments give way to a more airy and solemn composition (BIRDS), where woodwinds and brass instruments are prevalent over strings and percussions, and the composer shows an extraordinarily complex ability in counterpoint reflection and elaboration (THE RIVER, THE EDGE). Goldsmith, in

---

[144] ROBERTO PUGLIESE, *Il primo cavaliere*, in "Segnocinema", no.77, January/February 1996, p.78.

short, though he never feared to work on "lower" movie genres, and in fact preferred them to "art house" cinema, still considers the most extreme and redundant action movies as a chance to experiment with a "frontier" orchestra, expertly mixed with synthetics and making wide use of percussions, without betraying his old "tools of the trade": in a sense, this is a defiantly nostalgic answer to the bland *techno* seriality of many current movie scores.[145]

Pugliese's words gather a significant element in Goldsmith's conception of musical research within commissioned work: his openness towards new sounds through the use of peculiar instruments, and the conscious and integrated use of synthetic computer sounds, without disregarding the possibilities offered by a symphonic orchestra. One of Goldsmith's few works for Disney is the animated movie *Mulan* (1998), which moves away from the typical dramatic and musical schematics of the "House of Mouse". Goldsmith approaches the topic as he would do with a regular adventure movie:

> Goldsmith's score is remarkable, first and foremost, for its drastic refusal of Eastern exoticism: the movie's main theme (ATTACK AT THE WALL), on the contrary, shows the typical beat and rhythm of a Western-style ride, especially in its brash presentation of horns. Some element of Orientalism can be detected in MULAN'S DECISION, while the sweet princess theme is entrusted to the woodwinds in BLOSSOMS; the atmospheres of THE HUNS ATTACK and THE BURNED-OUT VILLAGE, on the other hand, are defined through a spare and lyrical use of strings and the faraway mixture of woodwinds.[146]

Later, Goldsmith went back to a horror-adventure *pastiche* with *The Mummy* (1999; directed by Stephen Sommers), a score showing a considerable orchestral undertaking, imposing and technically remarkable, once again used on a movie which does not manage to reach a very impressive result:

> Jerry Goldsmith's second youth is unstoppable, once again displayed in

---

[145] ID., *L'urlo dell'odio/Deep Rising*, in "Segnocinema", no.92, July/August 1998, p.78.

[146] ID., *Mulan*, in "Segnocinema", no.94, November/December 1998, p.78.

the movie genres that are traditionally more congenial to him: horror and adventure. (...). Besides its usual, amazing orchestral color (Iмноте, Nɪɢнт Boarders), *The Mummy* is remarkable for a careful and never gratuitous use of exotic-Arabian material in the magnificent main theme and the scathing incursions of modern solutions (Reвɪктн), often resulting from a slippery use of strings and drilling bass perorations. A dazzling example of 'horror music', sunny in its own way and, as always, superintended by the fierce organization of Goldsmith's rhythm.[147]

Ironically, Goldsmith himself had a less-than-flattering opinion on the movie's dramatic result, which he basically defined as childish and botched, so much that "he [had] never been so depressed in his life as when he was writing [this score]".[148] Perhaps this was one of the reasons why Goldsmith's younger colleague Alan Silvestri, a regular collaborator of director Robert Zemeckis, was later hired to write the music for the movie's 2002 sequel. Shortly after *The Mummy,* in the span of a few short weeks, Goldsmith had to compose another score for Michael Crichton, a novelist and director he had already worked with during the 70s and '80s; the movie, directed by John McTiernan, was *The 13ᵗʰ Warrior*, a medieval adventure revolving around an Arabic ambassador on a mission among the Vikings, who ends up fighting a tribe of cannibals. Based on Crichton's novel *Eaters of the Dead* (1976), the movie's plot outlines the events later described in epic poem *Beowulf.* In spite of the little time available, Goldsmith's score was decent, although stylistically very close to some of his other works in the same vein, both older and more recent. We may notice some resemblance to the composer's "blueprint" adventure score *The Wind and the Lion*, as well as to *The Mummy*, released in the same year. This movie was plagued by shooting difficulties, due to lacks in the script and to a troubled direction; the latter, credited to McTiernan alone, was in great part the work of Crichton himself, as the author was unhappy with his colleague's results. Crichton, being also one of the movie's producers, was free to

---

[147] Iᴅ., *La mummia/The Haunting*, in "Segnocinema", no.100, November/December 1999, p.76.
[148] As reported during Goldsmith's London concerts in May 2000, in "Soundtrack! The collector's quarterly", vol.19, no.74, Summer 2000, p.20.

make changes in scoring as well: before contacting Goldsmith, he had hired New Zealander composer Graeme Revell – who actually wrote a whole score for the movie – and Lisa Gerrard, a vocalist who had worked with Hans Zimmer on *Gladiator*.

Western

As many other movie composers before him – both older and contemporary –, Goldsmith was catapulted into Hollywood's most successful movie genre right at the beginning of his career. His actual composing debut, in 1957, was in *Black Patch* (directed by Allen H. Miller), a mediocre, soon-forgotten Western. Goldsmith's presence in this genre was marked by a massive amount of work both in movie and in TV productions, as well as in radio shows from the early 1950s. Some of these were traditional westerns, such as *Rio Conchos* (1964; directed by Gordon Douglas), *Stagecoach* (1966; directed by Gordon Douglas; a remake of John Ford's *Stagecoach*, 1939), *Hour of the Gun* (1967; directed by John Sturges), *100 Rifles* (1968; directed by Tom Gries), *Bandolero!* (1968; directed by Andrew V.McLaglen), *Take a Hard Ride* (1975; directed by Anthony Dawson, *alias* of Antonio Margheriti), as well as the trite genre comeback *Bad Girls* (1994; directed by Jonathan Kaplan), and several episodes for TV shows. In *The Last Hard Men* (1976; directed by Andrew V.McLaglen) Goldsmith was credited for the use of some of his older pieces – from *Rio Conchos*, *100 Rifles*, *Morituri* and *Stagecoach* –, though he had not offered any original contribution (the movie's previous score, written by Leonard Rosenman, had been rejected by the production team). Other Western-style movies, less connected to this genre's stereotypes, are: *Lonely Are the Brave* (1962), *The Ballad of Cable Hogue* (1970), *Wild Rovers* (1971) as well as action-western hybrid *Breakheart Pass* (1975; directed by Tom Gries), which includes a typically "galloping" and rhythmic main theme. Clearly, when approaching Westerns, the composer was seldom able to dramatically express himself due to the specific nature of such products, targeted towards an unpretentious audience. A partial return to Goldsmith's peculiar style can be detected in the pressing rhythm of some motifs (the previously mentioned *Breakheart Pass*, as well as parts of *Hour of the Gun*, *Bandolero!* and *Stagecoach*) and the frequent "limping" character of others – such as the score for *Rio Conchos*. Goldsmith's trademark irregular themes are repeatedly found in the composer's following productions, often for different genres – action movies and the like – e.g. the previously mentioned *Capricorn One*, *Total Recall* and the Disney-produced *Night Crossing* (1981). The composer rarely performed his western scores in later *suites* or recording sessions – even after many years – with the exception of *Rio Conchos*, recorded with the London Symphony Orchestra and published in 1989 by American recording label Intrada. Goldsmith, like many of his colleagues, considered Western movies just a necessary step in his Hollywood career: they meant performing a lot of work in a very short time, especially when TV series were involved. Though Goldsmith's talent was rarely celebrated with awards, the U.S. movie industry chose to acknowledge one of his Western scores: he was awarded an Emmy for *The Red Pony* (1973; directed by Robert Totten), a new version of John Steinbeck's celebrated novel, after the classic 1949 movie directed by Lewis Milestone and enriched by Aaron Copland's music.

Drama and comedy

Few of Goldsmith's experiments in the dramatic genre are worth mentioning. Our attention immediately turns to a couple of scores from the composer's beginnings, such as *Freud* (1962) and *A Patch of Blue* (1965; directed by Guy Green), if only because they earned him professional acknowledgements such as his Oscar nominations. Both works, though very different from one another, mirror the composer's constant search for a diverse approach. *Freud,* one of John Huston's less successful movies, faced Goldsmith with the task of describing the world of psychoanalysis – a feat resulting in a brave example of musical language verging on atonality. The orchestra followed a puntillistic pattern, highlighting the strings through expressive phrasings – so often used in avant-garde music – such as *glissando, picchettati* and the more traditional *pizzicati*. A rather daring choice, considering the composer, at the time barely over 30 years old, had been hired to score a Universal-produced movie by a renowned director. Almost twenty years later, *Freud*'s score was considered apt to describe the shifty and dark outer space of *Alien* and used as a *temp-track* for this science-fiction movie.[149] More "relaxed" was the score for *A Patch of Blue*, a movie about a naïve, blind young woman oppressed by her mother and alcoholic grandfather, who believes she can escape her sad existence with the help of an African-American boy (played by Sidney Poitier). Goldsmith's approach to this score was uncharacteristically close to jazz, though the opening was dutifully and traditionally lyrical. As the movie is so full of dialogue, the score is unobtrusive and characterized by an almost chamber-like instrumentation; the main theme is initially performed by the piano alone, later joined by a solo violin. While *Freud* was all but forgotten during the composer's concerts and recording sessions,[150] the main theme for *A Patch of Blue* was included in a concert *suite* and, thanks to its simplicity in pattern and harmony, went on to become one of the most recognizable main themes in Goldsmith's career. A similar movie, also starring Sidney Poitier, was *Lilies of the Field* (1963; directed by Ralph Nelson): both this picture and *A Patch of Blue*, were part of a "new course" in melodrama: little opulence, minimalist plots and low budgets, as they were shot during the major studios' great financial crisis. Going back to Goldsmith's first scores we can find several passionate stories of love and death: *Studs Lonigan* (1960; directed by Irving Lerner), *The Spiral Road* (1962; directed by Robert Mulligan), *A Gathering of Eagles* (1963). All of them, mixing war movie and melodrama, recall a

---

[149] Although Goldsmith did not agree with this decision, three tracks of *Freud*'s score were used in *Alien*'s final score. The composer defined this *temp track* practice as the "kiss of death", as he believed a temporary presence of music to have an excessive influence on the client's expectations.

[150] Despite this score's good critical result, there is no official re-mastered recording; the only available version is an unofficial one, published in Germany by record label Tsunami. While for *Rio Conchos* and *The Sand Pebbles* Goldsmith, between 1989 and 1997, went back to the recording studio in order to restrain the illegal commercialization of these recordings, *Freud* was never considered worthy of similar measures.

dated tradition which the composer approached more out of necessity than moved by inspiration. In 1965 Goldsmith was hired to write the prologue to Carol Reed's movie *The Agony and the Ecstasy* (scored by his own friend and mentor Alex North); this contribution, aiming to briefly showcase Michelangelo Buonarroti's artistic activity in the Renaissance, consisted in a twelve-and-a-half minute long piece called *The Artist Who Did not Want to Paint*. Goldsmith created a sort of symphonic poem in five parts: 'Rome', 'Florence', 'The Crucifix', 'The Stone Giants' and 'The Agony of Creation'. The ensemble was formed by strings – a quartet is especially apparent – woodwinds, harp, light percussions and a brass section rich in horns. More interesting are Goldsmith's works from the 1970s, when the composer was still engaged in the last part of his TV experience, (between 1971 and 1975) which earned him his three Emmys. The two most remarkable movies of this phase are *QBVII* (1974) and *Babe* (1975). The first one is closely connected, as if in a dip-tych, to the following *Masada* (1981), which we already mentioned among Goldsmith's adventure movie works. *QBVII* and *Masada* represent the composer's longest scores, both well over six hours long, though half of the *Masada* score was assigned to another composer who reworked Goldsmith's material; their strongest connection, however, is given by their common Jewish theme, explored in different his-torical settings. *QBVII* – based on a novel by Leon Uris – recalls the Holocaust, allowing the composer to perform a musical reflection on the topic – the main theme, with the help of a choir, evolves in the piece A KADDISH FOR THE SIX MILLION, one of the most heartfelt moments in the musician's career; the second one, on the other hand, tackles the Jewish people's deep-rooted fight against the Roman invaders. The two scores allow the composer to express closeness to his family roots through music. Goldsmith's Jewish background is generally not so easy to connect to the rest of his work, which is mainly based on the study of European tradition and on the communication practice of American media. It is remarkable, however, how both soundtracks on this topic show a noticeable emotional participation. On the subject of *QBVII* we also have one of the composer's rare descriptions of his own music:

I can quite honestly say that QBVII was probably the greatest creative challenge I have ever faced. One central statement or theme was impossible for a drama of this scope and dimension. It was necessary to treat each part with its own identifying musical statement, a formidable task considering the number of elements involved, and the need to unify them over-all. The Main Title starts with a fanfare which is later used to depict the exterior of the Royal Court, then goes to the Kelno theme [Adam Kelno is the doctor accused of practicing his profession for the use of the Nazi regime *a/n*], followed by the Cady theme [writer Abe Cady, Dr Kelno's accuser, played by Ben Gazzara, *a/n*] and ends with a re-statement of the fanfare. The love theme for Cady and Samantha (Juliet Mills), I Cannot See My Love, is a variation on the Cady theme in a major key. How to treat the subject of the concentration camps and human suffering was a difficult problem. Musically, there had to be pain, but yet culmination in a feeling of hope. I used the text of the Kaddish, the Jewish mourners' prayer, as the words to this theme. The words, in Hebrew, were sung abstractly (The Holocaust), spoken abstractly (Jadwiga Relived), and sung purely (A Kaddish for the Six Million). The music for the building of a new Israel (Rekindling the Flame of Jehovah) is that of *Hora*, the national dance of Israel.[151] The new love relationship between Cady and Lady Margaret (Lee Remick) is defined purely romantically (Free to Love Again). For me, the drama of QBVII is more than entertainment. It is a plea to mankind for love and tolerance towards their fellowman – a plea that is both personal and deeply felt by me.[152]

Babe, an intimist score showing little intervention over the *mezzoforte*, delicately accompanies the tragic story of sporting champion Babe Didrikson Zacharias, a two-time gold medal winner at the 1932 Olympics and a great athlete who competed in many different sports. The melodramatic side of her story, on which the movie is mainly focused, is the

---

[151] '[The actual *hora*] is a Romanian popular dance in ternary rhythm. Usually played slowly, it encourages the player to improve it through virtuosism. It is also known as *zhok* and it's strictly not to be confused with the modern *hora*, the lively Israeli dance going by the same name.' In Gabriele Coen, Isotta Toso, *Klezmer! - La musica popolare ebraica dallo shtetl a John Zorn*, Rome, Castelvecchi, 2000, p.226.

[152] Jerry Goldsmith, cover notes to *QBVII – Original Soundtrack Recording* - CD Intrada Maf-7061D, 1995.

115

cancer that struck her when she was 42, leading to her death in 1956. After leaving television in 1975, Goldsmith devoted himself exclusively to movies. A successful cinematic experiment in drama was *Islands in the Stream* (1977; directed by Franklin J. Schaffner), based on the posthumous Ernest Hemingway novel published in 1970. The composer expressed his satisfaction with the final result of this score – his favorite, among his works – so much that in 1986, not a decade after its creation, he decided to record it again in order to avoid the proliferation of unauthorized versions. About this score, he said:

> [My favorite score is] Franklin J.Schaffner's *Islands in the Stream*. (...) Without a doubt, the music for this film is some of the best I have written. Because the picture did not enjoy the promotion it deserved, its life at the box-office was short lived and the soundtrack existed only in a poor 'pirated' version. When I was approached by Intrada Records [ten years after the original première] to re-record this music in digital sound I jumped at the chance. I felt that the original recording, both in the recording and playing, could have been better (...). I would be recording Schaffner's newest film, *Lionheart* [1987, a/n] Since Frank would be with me, I suggested that he participate as Executive Producer. He agreed and sessions were set for the first weekend following the recording of *Lionheart*. We were all terribly tired after the work on *Lionheart*, but with the opening surge of low woodwinds and 'Hudson's theme' played by the solo French Horn, we found a new energy [the theme for the main character, Thomas Hudson, played by George C. Scott; a/n]...[153] perhaps like a visit with an old and long lost friend. From the first viewing of a 'rough cut' to my last screening just a few days ago, a period of time during which my emotional ties to this film have grown deeper and stronger. With that growth came an even greater appreciation for the art of Franklin J.Schaffner, and the beauty of *Islands in the Stream*.[154]

Later on, Goldsmith's work on drama became less frequent, including

---

[153]   The musical reference described by Goldsmith can be heard on the score's first track, THE ISLAND.

[154]   JERRY GOLDSMITH, cover notes to *Islands in the Stream- Original Motion Picture Score*, CD Intrada Rvf-6003D, 1986.

the composition of *Raggedy Man* (1981; directed by Jack Fisk), *Love Field* (1991; directed by Jonathan Kaplan and released two years later), *Not without My Daughter* (1991; directed by Brian Gilbert), *Forever Young* (1992; directed by Steve Miner), *Angie* (1995; directed by Martha Coolidge). There are a few remarkable pages but, overall, Goldsmith's contribution is purely functional and does not add anything to his remaining body of work.[155] *The Russia House* (1990; directed by Fred Schepisi), a mixture of melodrama and spy fiction based on the post-Cold War novel by John Le Carré, shows a melodically remarkable main theme – which, as many of the composer's "love themes", is tinged with melancholy – thus highlighting the affair between the main characters (Sean Connery and Michelle Pfeiffer) rather than the plot's international intrigue. The movie's main theme was based on a previous piece, written for science fiction movie *Alien Nation* (1988) and never used in the movie's final version.

Goldsmith's work on comedies started immediately: between 1963 and 1973 he was hired for about ten projects, after which he abandoned the genre until the 1980s; later on, the collaboration with director Joe Dante stimulated the composer's parodistic, if not strictly comical, side. Right at the beginning of his career, Goldsmith was hired for a few parodies of the spy genre: *The Prize* (1963; directed by Mark Robson) and the two agent Flint movies starring James Coburn – *Our Man Flint* (1965; directed by Daniel Mann) and *In Like Flint* (1966; directed by Gordon Douglas). While working on these scores, based on a lighter orchestration for a less opulent result, Goldsmith approached the style of composers more attuned than him to this genre, such as Henry Mancini, who wrote several "light" scores like those for the *Pink Panther* series (starting in 1964). However, while Mancini's comedy scores became his trademark, Goldsmith never felt completely at ease when writing them; their final result, especially in the movies about 'anti-James Bond' agent Flint, brings to mind a sort of amusing musical experiment. The composer later accepted a few similar assignments,

---

[155] Out of these titles, only the Love Theme from Forever Young was 'saved' and performed during concerts.

handling them with professionalism: *Take Her, She's Mine* (1963; directed by Henry Koster) and *The Trouble with Angels* (1965; directed by Ida Lupino). Less comedic and more grotesque were the scores for *The Flim-Flam Man* (1967; directed by Irvin Kershner) and *The Traveling Executioner* (1970; directed by Jack Smight). In 1982, after his "heavy" works from the 1970s, Goldsmith went back to a lighter tone with his first cartoon feature, *The Secret of N.I.M.H.* (1982; directed by Don Bluth). For this project, rather than a proper "comedic" score, he created an impressionistic palette with Debussy-inspired atmospheres – as he had previously done, though with a different intent, for *Alien*; to better underline its nature as a children's story, the movie was interspersed with more relaxed songs written with Paul Williams. Some of *N.I.M.H.*'s pieces, however, are still to be considered among Goldsmith's best. The score is one of Goldsmith's most interesting efforts: just like Goldsmith's "adult" music for *Mulan*, which the composer treated like a regular adventure movie by mixing nostalgia, romance and humor with moments of tension, *N.I.M.H*'s score is important because it strives to give a higher musical dignity to an animated movie.

After their first two purely comedic collaborations, *Gremlins* (1984) and *Innerspace* (1987), director Joe Dante and Goldsmith veered towards the grotesque with *The 'Burbs* (1988), the *Gremlins* sequel (1990) and *Matinee* (1992). Goldsmith's other commissions from this period were lackluster, even from a musical point of view: *Rent-a-Cop* (1988; directed by Jerry London), *Mr.Baseball* (1992; directed by Fred Schepisi) and *Mom and Dad Save the World* (1992; directed by Greg Beeman). *Dennis the Menace* (1993; directed by Nick Castle), on the other hand, is a remarkable study in instrumental comedic characterization, turning Wagner's trademark brass – the tuba – into a solo instrument, and highlighting the role of the harmonica: a study in orchestration rather than in musical invention, but an entertaining one nonetheless. Another, more peculiar comedy is *Six Degrees of Separation* (1993; directed by Fred Schepisi), based on John Guare's theatrical play; the composer's work here is more sparse as the movie is full of dialogue, though it is noticeable for the composition of a well-written tango. Amidst the epic-adventurous movies from 1995-1997 we find two more remarkable comedy scores, both verging on the grotesque: the mellow score – highlighting the piano – for *Fierce Ceatures* (1996; directed by Fred Schepisi and Robert Young), a sequel to the more successful *A Fish Called Wanda* (1987); and the one for *Two Days in the Valley* (1996; directed by John Herzfeld), an overall commendable ensemble comedy: once more, in this case, Goldsmith's music was rejected and replaced with a score written by lesser-known composer Anthony Marinelli.[156]

The year 2003 marked the composer's return to comedy, with the musical citationism and entertainment of *Looney Tunes: Back in Action* (directed by Joe Dante); this movie, just like its predecessor *Who Framed Roger Rabbit?* (1988; directed by Robert Zemeckis), showed human actors sharing the scene with Warner Bros' classic cartoon characters.

It is understandable that a composer who lived much of his professional life within the Hollywood industry should adapt to the most varied commissions, proving his extreme eclecticism and lack of snobbery. Goldsmith had the merit of not confining himself to the values of his musical education, influenced by the most significant novelties of the 20th century; much of his spirit of adaptation certainly came from his professional beginnings and his experience in popular radio and television. In the movie production system, by nature inclined to compromise, the composer nevertheless managed to offer his personal contribution, by combining his seasoned technique with an inspiration keeping pace with the most advanced musical conquests of the 20th century.

---

[156] Goldsmith's original score for this movie can be heard on its unofficial edition. The commercialized DVD, however, only includes the new version of the score.

4
IN THE *STAR TREK* SAGA

The conclusion of Goldsmith's *Alien* experience, marked by a prolonged debate on composing choices, was closely followed by another science-fiction work, which proved just as demanding but had far less controversial results. The score for the first episode in the *Star Trek* movie saga was created in a distinctly more peaceful environment: Goldsmith was once more working with Robert Wise, a director he had met before while scoring *The Sand Pebbles* (1966).

It was the first in a series of movies meant to revive and rehash the eponymous 1960s American TV show.[157] Goldsmith himself, while commenting on images from the first movie, explained almost too candidly what he believed to be the two possible approaches to science fiction:

> When it came to *Star Trek: The Motion Picture*... although I think that George Lucas's visioning of the music for *Star Wars* greatly influenced not so much what John Williams wrote, stylistically the music, rather than being avant-garde and strange, is very romantic. When you think about it, space is very romantic. To me, it's like the old west. We're up in the endless universe. It's about discovery, new life. When it came to the basic premise of *Star Trek*. I never understood all the stories, to be honest. But I did know it's about goodness. It's about a better world where we can live in peace and tranquility with one another. It's a lovely thought. That's the universal appeal of it. Musically, you'll go that way. (...) It made sense. I've treated all the *Star Trek* movies that I've done in this more musically romantic way, rather than getting very avant-garde and making strange noises. It's the opposite approach from *Planet of the Apes*.[158]

---

[157] After the end of the science-fiction movie saga, several new TV series followed the adventures of the Enterprise, albeit with different characters: among them, *Star Trek: the Next Generation*, *Star Trek: Voyager*, *Star Trek: Deep Space Nine* and *Star Trek: Enterprise* were particularly remarkable. Goldsmith created an original main theme for *Voyager*, while other composers (especially Dennis McCarthy) worked on the remaining shows. The main theme from the first *Star Trek* movie went on to become the title theme for *Star Trek: The Next Generation*.

[158] Transcrip. of Goldsmith's commentary on the *Star Trek: The Motion Picture* DVD, *op.cit.*

Although *Alien* referred to cosmic infinity as a source of new knowledge, in the name of a universal brotherhood that *Star Trek* would later tout as a value, Goldsmith's approach to Ridley Scott's movie, a contemporary of the first *Star Trek* episode, was extremely different: rather than symbolizing excitement for the discovery of different life forms, *Alien*'s universe was a source of ancestral fear. Two main approaches to science-fiction movies co-existed in the composer's mind: one was linked to *Planet of the Apes*; the other, to the first *Star Trek* movie; *Alien* mostly belongs to the first approach. Here's how the composer recalls an anecdote connecting him to the original *Star Trek* TV show, on air more than 10 years before the movie's release:

> The original *Star Trek*, the television show, I was asked to do it originally. Alexander Courage tells this story. He reminded me of it, as a matter of fact. He'd seen a memo from Roddenberry to try and engage me for that. I remember to this day, some 30 years ago, getting a phone call to do it. I was unable to do it. I had a conflict. I was doing something else. It's serendipitous that years later, I came back to this project.[159]

For this particular movie, Goldsmith drafted a few pages forming the score's thematic framework, including the main theme which would later become the 'Enterprise-theme' (and which can be found in the Mᴀɪɴ Tɪᴛʟᴇ):

[*Star Trek: The Motion Picture* (1979), 'Enterprise-theme']

Much as the theme is well-known, due to its many adaptations on television and records, its birth was anything but simple. While referring to the scene of the spaceship's departure, director Robert Wise recalled

---

[159] *Ibid.*

the days of its composing process:

> He started recording music before he came up with that theme [The Enterprise theme, a/n]. He did five or six cues in September '79. He used them against the picture and they didn't work. This cue (...) was one of them. The love theme was in place, but the main theme was undeveloped. I called a few people to hear the music. Everyone agreed it didn't work, so I had to tell Jerry. Fortunately, we broke for a month while we got more effects in it. Jerry hit upon the theme. When they came back at the end of October, he recorded new versions of those cues. When we did the director's cut, we took the original music scoring tapes and remixed them digitally, so it sounds as good as it can be.[160]

As the movie was rushed for a December 1979 release, some of its features were overlooked, so much that Wise candidly admitted:

> Thank goodness we had Jerry's score. I told him that music would take the place of sound effects. He really saved us.[161]

The musical aspect of the movie is actually substantial, often serving as a substitute for dialogues or mere sound effects. One remarkable example in this sense is the "cloud sequence" (track THE CLOUD): here, the Enterprise travels inside an entity which turns out to be emanated from an ancient space probe from Earth and is now "looking for its Creator".

Another significant sequence is represented by the spaceship's departure, underlined by the movie's main theme (LEAVING DRYDOCK). This scene caused Goldsmith quite a lot of trouble, as both the director and film editor felt the first version of the track to be too "descriptive", almost as if it belonged to a sea adventure modeled on Erich Wolfgang Korngold's *The Sea Hawk* (1940) or Miklós Rózsa's *All the Brothers Were Valiant* (1955) (which, in turn, were inspired by symphonic repertoire pieces). The composer had written a theme which, when heard today,

---

[160] Transcription of Robert Wise's commentary from the DVD, *op.cit.*, chapter 12.
[161] *Ibid.*

almost sounds like a variation on the final one.[162] We can guess, by the director's words, how often the composer was forced to find quick solutions, due to the tight schedule imposed by production. The two sequences we just described are, from a musical point of view, among the best in the whole movie. The soundtrack, however, includes several other themes that are just as well-rooted in its structure.

The track called Ilia's Theme – here employed as a 'love theme' of sorts – opens the movie almost like a "closed-curtain overture"; a different version of the track is later heard when navigator Ilia falls prey to the entity named V'ger, – or Vejur, as Goldsmith calls it in his score – though being an opening piece remains its main purpose:

[*Star Trek: The Motion Picture* (1979), 'Ilia-theme']

Because of its fifth-based pattern, the 'Klingon theme' (underlining, with a rhythmic pace provided by the grave parts of the orchestra, the opening scene where three aircrafts "crash" against the enemy's cloud) is closely reminiscent of the third movement (Scherzo, *Allegro molto*; m.21-25) from *Symphony #4 in F minor* (1935) by Ralph Vaughan-Williams (1872-1958):

[Ralph Vaughan-Williams, *Symphony #4 in F minor*, mov.III, b.21-25]

---

[162] A fragment of the sequence showing the departure of Enterprise can be seen in the documentary *A New Enterprise*, part of the aforementioned DVD.

Goldsmith's theme envisaged a rhythmic pattern of tubas and trombones as well as a grave string pizzicato, with a fundamental timbric help provided by Javanese rattles (*anklungs*) played as castanets. Against this background, the horn section draws a simple phrasing starting with two repeated notes, divided by a fifth:

[*Star Trek: The Motion Picture* (1979), 'Klingon theme']

The 'Vejur theme' is a two-note motto associated with the movie's villain. In this case, however, all music connected to the "enemy" is marked from a timbric rather than thematic point of view, thanks to the use of a peculiar percussion instrument called *blaster beam*.

Every main musical cell in this score returns as a reminiscence or in a different version; this especially applies to the first movie, although Goldsmith employed the same method (with the addition of new material and the exclusion of the 'Vejur theme') in every *Star Trek* sequel he scored.[163] Although – unlike *Star Wars* – the *Star Trek* movies were not planned as a saga from the start, the contribution of different composers meant that the movies, from a musical point of view, were somewhat uneven. The only constant piece, a sort of title theme for the

---

[163] The *Star Trek* movies Goldsmith did not work on are: *Star Trek II: The Wrath of Khan* (1982; directed by Nicholas Meyer and scored by James Horner); *Star Trek III: In Search of Spock* (1983; directed by Leonard Nimoy, and again scored by Horner); *Star Trek IV: The Voyage Home* (1987; directed by Leonard Nimoy and scored by Leonard Rosenman); *Star Trek VI: The Undiscovered Country* (1991; directed by Nicholas Meyer and scored by Cliff Eidelman); *Star Trek: Generations* (1994; directed by David Carson and scored by Dennis McCarthy). Jerry Goldsmith scored the saga's eighth movie, *Star Trek: First Contact* (1996; directed by Jonathan Frakes), though the composer's son Joel wrote a few additional pages and is thus credited as co-author.

saga, was the opening fanfare from the TV series' main theme, written by Alexander Courage. About the use of this brief musical "trademark", Goldsmith recounted:

> When I was asked, I said I'd love to do the movie, but on condition I wasn't saddled with the television theme. They said, "Fine. There's not going to be any association." How can you do Star Trek: The Motion Picture with William Shatner, Leonard Nimoy and all the cast and not be associated with the TV show? That's where it came from. Subsequently, there's one quote of the original Star Trek theme under the Captain's log. They decided they had to have it somewhere in the picture. I had Alexander Courage do it, which was the right way to go. In all the other Star Treks I've done, the four other films, I always start the film with the Sandy Courage fanfare from the TV show, which I think is right to do. And then go to the theme I wrote.[164]

Similarly, the composers who scored the other sequels (James Horner, Leonard Rosenman, Cliff Eidelman and Dennis McCarthy) brought their own personal touch while keeping in mind Courage's TV fanfare, which preludes to the actual, "dancing" theme of the movie. Goldsmith's main theme for the first movie, however, soon became another symbol of the saga, making an impression on the audience's imagination almost as much as Courage's TV theme had done.

About a decade later, the composer went back to score the fifth episode of the saga – Star Trek V: The Final Frontier (1989; directed by William Shatner). The score opened by using Courage's TV fanfare, and reworked several themes from the first movie. Goldsmith created a different version of the 'Klingon theme' as well, by applying a more incisive use of brass, additional percussions, pizzicato strings and ram's horn (a primitive instrument also appearing, as we previously mentioned, in the Planet of the Apes score). The score includes various other main themes, such as the one linked to Vulcan character Sybok, an alien who turns out to be Spock's half-brother; we also find a very evocative, descriptive piece associated to the mountain landscape where Cap-

---

[164] Transcription of Goldsmith's commentary from the Star Trek: The Motion Picture DVD, op.cit., chapter 16.

tain Kirk is sojourning on leave at the start of the movie (THE MOUNTAIN).[165] The return of the 'Klingon theme' is connected to a focal point in the plot: Sybok, a Vulcan with illusions of grandeur and the movie's token villain, has imprisoned a Klingon and a Romulian that are later saved by the heroes. The theme, however, is also linked to a crucial subplot, which shows the Klingon spaceship going in search of the Enterprise in order to kidnap Captain Kirk. The use of the Jewish liturgical horn, the *shofar* – or ram's horn – gives the 'Klingon theme' a stronger barbaric impact, as well as a touch of musical irony, due to the fact that the Klingon commander is shown as a caricature. The 'Klingon theme' can also be heard in WITHOUT HELP[166] (in the first movie's *regular* version and, later, in its new orchestration). Here's how Jeff Bond introduces the two parallel motifs connected to the movie's villain, and their relationship with the classic 'Enterprise theme':

> A four note motif for the Vulcan Sybok is introduced in the opening scene [THE MIND MELD]:[167] as a quirky, synthesized motif. [In RAID ON PARADISE] a new Sybok motif is introduced: also consisting of four notes, this theme is voiced by low brass and forms a rhythmic action motif that highlights the obsessive nature of Sybok's personality. The motif plays through the shuttle landing sequence, alternating with airy, flute-accented readings of the Enterprise theme and a restatement of (...) Klingon theme as a reneg-ade Bird of Prey attempts to target the starship.[168]

A second thematic reference – found, as we said, in track THE MOUNTAIN – creates a different, almost pastoral melodic center, underlining the friendship among the three main members of the crew.[169] The score for

---

[165] KESTER, *op.cit.*, p.30.

[166] Epic CD 476754-2, track#3. From 3'01" the track can be heard in its "Ram's horn" version.

[167] This piece is not included in the fragmented score selection, published by record label Epic, mirroring the saga's musical history.

[168] BOND, *The Music of Star Trek*, *op.cit.*, p.133-134.

[169] First track on the movie soundtrack album, but second sequence in a chronological order. A similar piece among Goldsmith's *Star Trek* scores is BA'KU VILLAGE in *Star Trek: Insurrection* (1998).

the series' fifth episode also possesses a strong mystic aura, due to the fact that the Enterprise voyage ends on a planet that Sybok describes as "God's home" (it is actually inhabited by a threatening and hostile entity that ends up killing him). The 'peace theme', symbolizing the ultimate harmony reached among humans, Romulians and Klingon, is first heard in track THE BARRIER.[170] The score's action tracks are OPEN THE GATES[171] and LET'S GET OUT OF HERE.[172] FREE MINDS,[173] on the other hand, is a descriptive interlude highlighting Sybok's power of persuasion on the three main characters. The score's conclusion, LIFE IS A DREAM, showcases, in close succession, the TV fanfare, the original version of the 'Klingon theme' and the 'Enterprise theme' in the first movie "marching" version; in its own way, therefore, it represents a connection to the saga's first movie.

Seven years later, Goldsmith returned to the Paramount-produced saga and reaffirmed his role as the Star Trek composer par excellence by scoring three consecutive sequels: *Star Trek: First Contact* (eighth sequel, 1996), *Star Trek: Insurrection* (ninth sequel, 1998) and *Star Trek: Nemesis* (tenth sequel, 2002); the first two were directed by Jonathan Frakes, one of the actors in the series, the third by Stuart Baird. None of the three movies shows a great expansion of the thematic component, as they mainly reuse themes from previous episodes. While composing the *First Contact* score, Goldsmith collaborated with son Joel, who wrote the sections connected to the movie's villains, the Borg. Goldsmith Sr., on the other hand, created a new main theme that can be heard right

---

[170] Track#2 in the Epic CD: the 'peace theme' can be heard from 1'20" until the end (interspersed by a hint of the TV fanfare). Track#4, A BUSY MAN, shows a more complete version of this theme from 1'41" until the end. Later on, in AN ANGRY GOD (track#6), from 1'21" to 3'03", the Sybok theme to grave brass takes the lead and the piece becomes more agitated.

[171] Epic CD, track#5. The sequence shows Kirk and his comrades, on planet Nimbus III, entering Paradise City on horses they stole from the sentinels.

[172] Epic CD, track#7. Here, the 'Klingon theme' returns in its original form; the track ends with a solemn version of the 'Enterprise theme'.

[173] Epic CD, track#8. The last track in the CD is actually from the middle of the movie, a scene where Sybok forces Kirk, Spock and McCoy to recall their most painful experiences.

after the trademark Courage fanfare, by then a distinctive trait of the series. The pace is solemn; the timbre is provided by horns:

[*Star Trek - First Contact* (1996), main theme]

> [The *First Contact* Main Theme], in cues like Main title and Welcome Aboard, reflects the *Star Trek* myth from a distance, rather than close-up. The music recognized the stature of its characters and their history, and speaks to this with veneration and admiration.[174]

Though several commentators appreciated The Dish, a dynamic, seven-minute piece in the footsteps of Goldsmith's traditional "chasing" music, the score did not receive many positive reviews, especially as far as the work of Joel Goldsmith was concerned:

> The contribution of Goldsmith's son Joel might be a point of interest, though it is very close to one of his previous works, *Moon 44*.[175] Several minor action themes from the first TREK feature also recur in cues like Red Alert and Retreat (the latter, by the way, is one of three cues composed by Goldsmith's son, Joel from Jerry's motifs).[176]

Perhaps counter-intuitively, the score's thematic sparseness was also criticized, although critics reaffirmed its good achievements in dramatic and functional terms. The following commentary mirrors some typ-

---

[174] Randall D. Larson, *Star Trek: First Contact*, in "Soundtrack!", vol.16 no.61, March 1997, p.30.

[175] Denis Bricka, *Star Trek: First Contact*, in "Soundtrack!", *ibid.*, p.3 (French edition).

[176] Randall D. Larson, *op.cit.*

ical contradictions from scholars of this subject. Movie scoring is created to be functional, and its very dignity is connected to this purpose, rather than to whether or not it may work outside of its prefixed context; if and when this manages to happen, it is largely due to the composition's inherent quality:

> The least successful aspect of the score is Goldsmith's attempt to bring so many differing musical elements together. There is a dearth of material. We have the original TV series fanfare, the *Star Trek: The Motion Picture* theme, the 'Angry God' motif from *Star Trek V*, the Klingon theme from Star Trek TMP, plus new Borg material and the new *First Contact* theme. Dramatically it works very well, but as a piece of music away from the film it just doesn't gel.[177]

For the saga's following chapter (1998), Goldsmith once more worked alone, with the orchestrating help of Alexander Courage. This score's most remarkable feature, especially when compared to the previous installments, is its mostly relaxed pattern. The opening piece BA'KU VILLAGE is uncharacteristically calm for a *Star Trek* movie; fragments of Courage's TV fanfare can be heard from subdued horns, until a solo harp introduces the new theme, a tender and captivating melody played by oboe, flutes and strings. The following harp rhythm gives the melody a "magical" aura. Slowly, the music grows in intensity and strength until it abandons its lyrical tone to enter a more percussive one, featuring a martial rhythm. The latter is then followed by a quiet phrasing of the main theme (the 'Enterprise theme'), closing the piece with a subtly noble tone, perfectly suited to the arrival of the spaceship and its crew. The main theme is later reprised in CHILDREN'S STORY by a murmuring harp, giving way to the appearance of woodwinds and to the surprising rise of the main theme by flute on violins, then by clarinet on harp. The melody is introspective and intimate, its opening rhythm provided by harp and pizzicato strings. NEW SIGHT reprises the lyrical tone of CHILDREN'S STORY with the soft timbre of woodwinds on

---

[177]   PAUL PLACE, *Star Trek: First Contact*, in "Music from the movies". No. 14/15, Spring 1997, p.25.

strings, creating undulating figurations. This piece expands the one and a half minute of the original to a total length of six minutes. The flute on harp turns the whole piece's subtle, melodic tenderness into a quiet reflection, finishing with violins taking the theme through a dazzling hemisphere of synthesized sounds. In the end, the forceful statement of brass and percussions, clashing with the previous sounds, closes the piece with sudden dynamism. The rest of the score consists in action pieces, impressive in spite of their excessive number. IN CUSTODY is an amazing and evocative string piece with quick figurations, hard percussion bursts and lacerating brass notes. NOT FUNCTIONING is a fierce action piece, its simple pattern amplified by echoing synthesized sounds. THE DRONES ATTACK[178] brings back the quickness of NOT FUNCTIONING with harsh phrasings of brass and percussions. The music is dissonant without abandoning its tonality, chaotic without losing its musical cohesion. All through the score, Goldsmith's echoing, heroic brass notes, not unlike the movie's heroes, hold the whole vortex together. THE RIKER MANEUVER, THE SAME RACE and NO THREAT are other action pieces in the same vein. At the end of THE HEALING PROCESS[179] the action motifs veer towards a tranquil and pastoral theme, as a pleasant woodwind melody provides an "antidote" (hence the track's title) to the more violent parts of the score, and a spiritual and musical regeneration brings the piece – and the movie – to a close. A final assertion of the 'Enterprise theme' emerges from the rolling kettledrums at the very end of the track, and the END CREDITS reprise the theme for the orchestral epilogue in the finale. *Insurrection* combines a single romantic melody with a series of tonal dissonances and, unlike the other movies in the series,

---

[178] The track THE DRONES ATTACK (which includes a subtle, yet effective reminiscence of the first movie's 'Klingon theme') was inspired by a different piece written by Goldsmith in 1990: MASSACRE, from *Total Recall*. This was first pointed out by PAUL PLACE's *Star Trek: Insurrection*, in "Music from the movies", No. 22, Winter 1999, p.20-21. Denis Bricka also indicates *Total Recall* as a model for the action pieces in this *Star Trek*; chapter quot. in DENIS BRICKA, *Star Trek: Insurrection*, in "Soundtrack!", vol.18 no.69, Spring 1999, p.5 (French edition).

[179] THE HEALING PROCESS, on the other hand, has some traits in common with a track from the first movie, THE CLOUD; quoted in PAUL PLACE, *ibid.*

does not show a prevailing thematic center, making it the saga's least approachable chapter.[180]

The references to previous Goldsmith works in this score were highlighted by several scholars, as the music was reviewed in specialized magazines. Besides *Total Recall*, Goldsmith's work on *First Blood* (1982; directed by Ted Kotcheff) was also cited as inspiration:

> THE RIKER MANEUVER showcases the composer's ability in dramatic construction, and the piano counterpoint effects in NO THREAT can't help but evoke *First Blood*.[181]

The last Goldsmith-scored chapter in the saga, *Star Trek: Nemesis*, was released in 2002 and is almost universally considered weak from both a cinematic and dramatic point of view. From a musical point of view it may be described as:

> a sort of chrestomathy of music from the previous episodes, widely reprising the original theme from Wise's movie and expertly mixing together orchestral and electronic effects. We find a recurrence of Goldsmith's famous syncopated marches and of his unforgettable experimental boldness, while Wagner's influence can be heard in the imposing orchestration and in the prevalence of brass instruments (REMUS, RIGHT ARM). The lyrical openings (REPAIRS) are gorgeous as per usual, and we find some harmonic passages of extraordinary dramatic power.[182]

Several years elapsed between Goldsmith's work on the first, second and third movie in the saga (ten years between episodes 1 and 2; seven between episodes 2 and 3). Outside of the cinematic context, however, the composer followed the adventures of the Enterprise and its crew by contributing to a new TV show, an ideal continuation of the one on air between 1966 and 1969. *Star Trek: The Next Generation* started in 1987 and was on air until 1994. The 1979 main theme became the new

---

[180] Description is based on: RANDALL D. LARSON, *Star Trek: Insurrection*, in "Soundtrack!", vol.17 no.68, Winter 1998-1999, out of text.

[181] DENIS BRICKA, *op.cit.*

[182] ROBERTO PUGLIESE, *Star Trek: Nemesis*, in "Segnocinema", no.123, September/October 2003, p.96.

show's title theme and symbol, an anthem of sorts to the saga, matching the popularity of Courage's famous TV fanfare. In 1995, for the new *Star Trek: Voyager* show (on air until 2001), Goldsmith wrote a new, short and solemn theme – similar to the *First Contact* theme, written one year later –, thus adding a new mosaic tile to his connection to the *Star Trek* world:

[*Star Trek: Voyager* (1995), main theme]

Star Trek's first movie: details in instrumentation

The *Star Trek: The Motion Picture* orchestra is imposing both in dimension and diversification, especially among percussions. Employed instruments are listed below, according to family:

Woodwinds: 3 flutes (3rd also piccolo); 3 clarinets (3rd also bass clarinet); 3 oboes (3rd also English horn); 3 bassoons (3rd contrabassoon); double bass clarinet; tenor sax; electronic alto flute; electronic bass flute with echoplex effect.[183]

---

[183] This instrument produces a flute-like sound accompanied by decreasing reverberations; its sound can be appreciated at the beginning of track KLINGON BATTLE. The instrument's reverberating effect was often used in the '60s and '70s, and Goldsmith

Brass: 4 trumpets; 6 horns; 4 trombones; 2 tubas.

Percussions: kettledrums; vibraphone; xylophone; marimba; glock-
enspiel; tubular bells; bass drum; cymbals; sizzle cymbals; tam-tams;
tom-toms; two wooden slit drums (a big one and a medium one); African log drums;[184] military drum; boo-bams;[185] triangle; blaster beam; rub
rods; song bells; water crotales; waterphones (both big and small);[186]
angklungs [Javanese bamboo rattles]; mixing bowls [round metal kitchen bowls]; wind machine; water chimes; rumble road;[187] bullroarer.

Strings : violins I; violins II; violas; cellos; double basses.[188]

Also: 2 harps; piano; electric piano; celesta; clavichord; harpsichord;
organ; electronic keyboards (CS-80; Arp 2600; OBX; Serge).

Among percussions we also find the so-called *Blaster Beam*, an instrument created by Craig Huxley (thus also known as a *Huxley Beam*)
shortly before this score was written.

The composer mentions the Blaster Beam in his audio commentary
to the movie's DVD edition:

> Paramount said: 'This guy's got this thing called a beam, let's go and listen
> to it.' It was a 12-foot-long piece of aluminum with strings on, metal
> strings strung the whole way over, and amplifiers under each string. You

---

had sometimes employed it while creating the initial trumpet figuration in *Patton* (only the first three notes are played, the rest being provided by the Echoplex); the reverberating piano in *Coma* (1977) and the echoing string pizzicato in *Planet of the Apes* and *Alien*.

[184] Also known as *elephant drums*.

[185] *Boo-bams* or *boobams* (the name comes from a syllabic inversion of the word *bam-boo*) are tuned bongos wrapped in natural bamboo. They have been commonly used in Hollywood orchestras since the 1950s. Their modern versions use wooden or synthetic wrappings (the latter are called *octobans*)

[186] Created in 1967, they are made of steel and bronze, and their shape is similar to a water-filled vase covered by a dome of sticks and tubes; they are played with the help of a bow.

[187] Also known as *thunder sheet*.

[188] According to Cameron N. Patrick's dissertation *Anatomy of a Film Score: Star Trek: The Motion Picture*, University of Queenslands, 1986, a standard distribution is used in this section: 28 violins (presumably 14+14), 10 violas, 10 cellos and 6 basses.

play it by hitting it with an artillery shell. Then you'd pump up the low end on the mixing console. It made rather an incredible noise. And quite musical, too. As you moved this shell, it was like how a steel-guitar player plays with his metal bar. It's the same process. You move that shell around and you hit it in different ways. You can hit the shell with the tip of a mallet. I got some interesting sounds. I got intrigued with it. So I said: 'I'll use that for the sound of V'Ger'. Bob [director Robert Wise] loved it.[189]

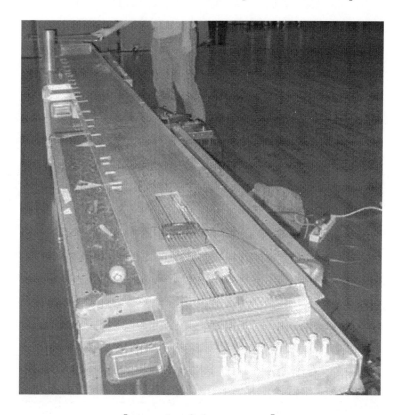

[Example of Blaster Beam]

---

[189] A transcription of the audio comment made by Goldsmith on chapter 17 of the DVD, *op.cit*. This instrument, capable of emitting peculiarly shrill sounds, usually appears together with an organ.

Robert Wise also mentioned the use of this and other unusual instruments, comparing his experience with Goldsmith to the one he'd had with Bernard Herrmann, another great name in science-fiction scoring:

> Jerry liked interesting sounds and non-traditional instruments to add to the usual symphony orchestra. There are a lot in the score for *Star Trek*: waterfalls, rubber boards, tune logs. He really created a unique sound for the picture. When I did *The Day the Earth Stood Still* [1951], Bernard Herrmann used a theremin on the score. It became associated with that film and with science fiction in general. The same thing happened with the blaster beam in this film.[190]

As the composer himself stated, the blaster beam was employed to underline the appearance of the enemy of starship Enterprise, the blurred image of the Vejur (or V'ger):[191] whenever the cloud-shaped villain appeared or hovered on the scene, Goldsmith chose to highlight it through the timbre of this peculiar percussion instrument, rather than by using a specific theme or rhythm. The blaster beam appears right in the opening sequence, the Klingon Battle,[192] a piece showcasing a veritable selection of percussive instrumentation (blaster beam, rumble road, slit drum, boo-bams and waterphones as well as electronic instruments such as Serge and Obx) and in Total Logic; later, halfway through the movie, the blaster beam appears in various tracks – Vejur Flyover, Force Field, Games e The Meld – culminating in The Cloud, a fight sequence involving the heroes and the villain. A few of these percussion instruments (*angklung*, sizzle cymbals, boo-bams, bullroarer, slit drum, waterphone, water chimes, wind effect and rumble road) are briefly described below. Goldsmith had previously used some of them, such as

---

[190] Robert Wise's commentary on chapter 17 of the DVD.

[191] The entity's name is spelled as Vejur in the score track's titles, though in the movie it is reported as 'V'ger', a preferable version considering the events that explain the origin of its name.

[192] In this scene, the battle sequence between the Klingon war ships and the V'ger cloud is marked by an opposition between the Klingon theme rhythm and the timbre of the blaster beam, which is the musical symbol of the 'Vejur'.

the *angklung* and boo-bams, in *Planet of the Apes*, where they had played a pivotal role in track The Hunt.

Angklung. A traditional Indonesian bamboo instrument. Each *angklung* provides the melody with its own sound (which the natives call a '*kling-klung*'), and these instruments can produce, on different octaves, the sounds of the four- and five-tone scale. The *Angklung* is entirely made out of bamboo reeds, and its construction is quite complex: it is formed by two, three or four carved reeds, in the shape of flaps, cut lengthwise (from a quarter-length of the reed until its upper extremity); underneath, near the knot, there is a small rail. A hole in the upper part of each reed (about a quarter-length from the tip) permits the introduction of a crosspiece, connected to a vertical frame formed by thicker or thinner reeds and attached to a small horizontal reed working as a base; small slits are carved lengthwise through the reed on this frame, allowing the reed to slide through the rail. No dynamic variation is possible.[193]

Sizzle cymbals. First employed in the age of *Dixieland* music. The best sizzle cymbals are thick and heavy, allowing for a certain consistency of sound, slow in their reaction to percussions, but, once the sound has started, producing intense and long-lasting vibrations, particularly on the edge.[194]

Boo-bams. A series of sound-determined membraphones hailing from Indonesia (West Java), they are a recent and valuable acquisition among Western percussion instruments. Their sound is similar to marimbas or single-skin tuned tom-toms, shrill and piercing, and is created by hitting them with hard knockers. Their dynamic range goes from *p* to *ff*, according to the percussive medium employed.[195]

The *Bull roarer* is a xylo aerophone. Widespread in Africa, Australia, Melanesia and Indonesia, this instrument is quickly spun above head producing a strong, deep hiss similar to a mooing sound. Its shrillness varies according to the size of the board and its speed of rotation.[196]

---

[193] Guido Facchin, *op.cit.*, p.310.
[194] *Ibid.*, p.84-85.
[195] *Ibid.*, p.577.
[196] *Ibid.*, p.684.

Slit drum a very ancient, possibly Paleolithic instrument, found on every continent except Europe. In Melanesia and Polynesia such instruments, usually played in a group, are built by carving the upper part of huge tree-trunks (up to ten meters long); after being emptied through a fist-sized slit, the trunks are fastened to the ground over a hole or placed on pieces of wood. Though this drum's sound pitch is easier to determine, especially when compared to similar instruments, the slit drum should be regarded as an undetermined intonation instrument, and its registers are simply defined as *high, medium, low-medium,* etc. The drum's dynamic range goes from *p* to *ff*.[197]

The *waterphone* is built by soldering together two kitchen pots or pans (minus the handles) in order to form a sounding-board containing a small quantity of water, with brass bars attached to the sides. The instrument works by pouring water inside the container and hitting the bars (with a light stick covered in rubber) while at the same time shaking the waterphone in order to move the water around. The resulting sound effect is grave, with an added glissando.[198]

Water chimes. In the Far East, water chimes are used not as musical instruments, but as lucky charms. The original version of this instrument is formed by a certain number of brass tubes (usually five or six) about 10 to 18 centimeters long and 7-9 millimeters wide. The tubes are hanged with strings to a special, crown-shaped round support. When used in an orchestra, they are made to vibrate with hands or metal sticks and produce a sweet, rhythmically irregular shrill tingle. Liza Lim, in her *Anactoria*, defines water-chimes as a cluster of five wind chimes in water. Their dynamic range grows exponentially with the number of chimes used.[199]

Wind machine. Mechanical devices imitating the sound of the wind have been in use since the 17th century. One such type of machine is formed by a faceted wooden cylinder, with raised edges, resting on a base frame. One side of a strip of cloth is attached to the side of the frame

---

[197]   *Ibid.*, p.292-294.
[198]   *Ibid.*, p.704.
[199]   *Ibid.*, p.16-17.

and, in order to keep it stretched, the opposite loose side is tied to a hanging weight. When the cylinder is rotated by the action of a handle, the facets rub against the cloth producing a higher or lower pitched hiss according to the speed of movement impressed on the handle.[200]

Thundersheet. Long employed in theatres as a special sound effect for rainstorm scenes, this device recently became part of orchestral pieces as well. It is formed by a rectangular steel, copper or tin sheet, of medium thickness and about 0.5x1 to 1x2 meters in size. Every dynamic effect is possible, from *pp* to *ff*, as well as *sforzando*, *crescendo* and *diminuendo*. In order to obtain stronger dynamics, the use of an amplifier is advisable.[201]

The remarkable feature in this score, therefore, lies not in its use of normal instruments – much as they can be strengthened – such as brass (though woodwinds are prominently featured as well, with the presence of two electrical flutes and a double bass clarinet), but in its percussive selection and the sparing, though effective, use of electronics.

---

[200] *Ibid.*, p.734. Also used in symphonies and opera. Richard Strauss used it in his *Don Quixote op.35* (1898) – *Fantastic Variations on a Theme of Knightly Character* –, for cello, viola and orchestra, namely in the 7th variation, *Der Ritt durch die Luft* (*The Ride through the Air*).

[201] *Ibid.*, p.40.

Appendix
Rejected scores

Finally, our attention turns to the peculiar issue, not so unusual in the film industry, that occurs when a score, written by a composer under contract for a certain movie, is rejected by the production team (sometimes with the director's approval): these so-called *rejected scores* briefly see the light, only to fall back into the shadows as the so-called *replaced scores* take their place. The unused scores, however, often find their own way to capture the audience's attention, especially as in most cases they are by no means second-rate works, and are usually perfectly enjoyable on record. The rejection of a whole score rarely raises an uproar outside of the production context – there are dozens of very well-known such cases; at the same time, however, gathering information about it is no easy feat. The first significant example of this phenomenon broke up the artistic relationship between Alfred Hitchcock and Bernard Herrmann, one of the most relevant associations in modern cinematography, which had until then produced a series of cinematic – and musical – masterpieces; the cause for the break-up was the 1966 score for *Torn Curtain*, for which Hitchcock demanded a catchy tune, a pop song to be released as a commercial vehicle for the movie. Herrmann, on the other hand, had firmly opposed any commercialization of his composing ability in the course of his whole career. It is said that Hitchcock did not enjoy listening to the score Herrmann had written – not so much for aesthetic reasons, but because he felt it was a testament to his colleague's stubbornness. Hitchcock rejected the music, cut off the collaboration, and hired another musician, John Addison, to score the movie. A few years later there was a similar, well-known episode, this time related to the use of a temporary score. We are referring to the most emblematic science-fiction film in movie history: *2001: A Space Odyssey* (1968) directed by Stanley Kubrick.[202] While editing the movie, Kubrick had employed some repertoire pieces of

---

[202] Sergio Bassetti, *La musica secondo Kubrick*, Turin, Lindau, 2002, p.81-98. On North's rejected score, see p.85-86.

139

concert music as a temporary score: the introduction to Richard Strauss' symphonic poem *Also sprach Zarathustra* (1896), Johann Strauss Jr's waltz *An der schönen blauen Donau* (*The Blue Danube*, 1867), the Adagio from Aram Khachaturyan's ballet *Gayaneh* (1942), as well as a contemporary piece first performed in 1961: *Atmosphères*, by György Ligeti.[203] As it was customary, the director hired a composer, in this case Alex North – a successful Hollywood musician capable of combining spectacular effects with a more nuanced approach – who had already worked with Kubrick on *Spartacus* (1960). North wrote the score in its entirety, drawing inspiration from some pieces that Kubrick had indicated as models. The director, however, seizing his first opportunity to be the *author* of every phase of his work (as he would later do in all of his movies), decided to reject North's work completely. Kubrick's decision caused a stir in the industry, not least because, as the story goes, the composer only found out about the rejection at the movie's first screening. Ever since then, in a remarkable turn of events, the director only scored his movies with classical pieces (Beethoven, Rossini and Elgar in *A Clockwork Orange*; Schubert and others in *Barry Lyndon*; Penderecki and Bartòk in *The Shining*), although in a couple of instances the pieces were electronically reworked by Wendy Carlos. For his last movie, *Eyes Wide Shut* (1999), Kubrick hired composer Jocelyn Pook to write a few specific tracks, which were amalgamated with selected works by Šostakovič and Ligeti.[204]

In past decades, however, the aforementioned cases of Herrmann and North were remarkable exceptions from the norm. Movie scores have been rejected or replaced more frequently in recent times, though it has not always happened so openly. The following chart includes a short list of the most famous rejected and replaced scores, merely shown by way of example.[205] The first, crossed-out name on the

---

[203] Kubrick had had some copyright trouble in using this piece. However, the director chose Ligeti for some of his following movies as well.

[204] Kubrick's death, in February 1999, left much doubt regarding the authorship of the movie's final editing and, consequently, its musical choices. *See*. Bassetti, *op.cit.*, p.157-172.

[205] Reports about rejected scores are sometimes conflicting. In other cases (e.g. the one

chart indicates the original composer of the rejected score, the second name indicates the composer chosen as a replacement.

Film	Original	Replacement
Seven Days in May (1964)	~~David Amram~~	Jerry Goldsmith
The Bible (1966)	~~Goffredo Petrassi~~	Toshirô Mayuzumi
Torn Curtain (1966)	~~Bernard Herrmann~~	John Addison
The Way West (1967)	~~Franz Waxman~~	Bronislau Kaper
2001: a Space Odissey (1968)	~~Alex North~~	Brani classici
Battle of Britain (1969)	~~William Walton~~	Ron Goodwin
The Reivers (1969)	~~Lalo Schifrin~~	John Williams
Frenzy (1972)	~~Henry Mancini~~	Ron Goodwin
The Getaway (1972)	~~Jerry Fielding~~	Quincy Jones
The Exorcist (1973)	~~Lalo Schifrin~~	Jack Nitzsche[206]
The Man Who Loved Cat Dancing (1973)	~~Michel Legrand~~	John Williams
Chinatown (1974)	~~Phillip Lambro~~	Jerry Goldsmith
S.P.Y.S. (1974)	~~John Scott~~	Jerry Goldsmith
Robin and Marian (1976)	~~Michel Legrand~~	John Barry
The Last Hard Men (1976)	~~Leonard Rosenman~~	Jerry Goldsmith[207]
Casey's Shadow (1978)	~~Elmer Bernstein~~	Patrick Williams
Neighbors (1981)	~~Tom Scott~~	Bill Conti
Wolfen (1981)	~~Craig Safan~~	James Horner
Five Days One Summer (1982)	~~Carl Davis~~	Elmer Bernstein
Journey of Natty Gann (1983)	~~Elmer Bernstein~~	James Horner
Streets of Fire (1984)	~~James Horner~~	Ry Cooder
Legend (1985)	~~Jerry Goldsmith~~	Tangerine Dream
Wall Street (1987)	~~Jerry Goldsmith~~	Stewart Copeland
Alien Nation (1988)	~~Jerry Goldsmith~~	Curt Sobel
Cocktail (1988)	~~Maurice Jarre~~	J.Peter Robinson
Dead Bang (1988)	~~Michael Kamen~~	Gary Chang
The Big Blue (1988)	~~Eric Serra~~	Bill Conti
Mobsters (1990)	~~Stewart Copeland~~	Michael Small
Gladiator (1992)	~~Jerry Goldsmith~~	Brad Fiedel
The Bodyguard (1992)	~~John Barry~~	Alan Silvestri
Jennifer Eight (1992)	~~Maurice Jarre~~	Christopher Young
A River Runs Through It (1992)	~~Elmer Bernstein~~	Mark Isham
The Public Eye (1992)	~~Jerry Goldsmith~~	Mark Isham

concerning Goldsmith's work on *Wall Street*) the composer's undertaking had merely been planned. For a very detailed and informed list, see: http://rejectedfilm-scores.150m.com/list.html.

[206] In addition to original music by Jack Nitzsche, also *Tubular Bells* by Mike Oldfield was included in the score.

[207] Goldsmith did not score new music for this movie. The production used his music from some previous westerns and from *Morituri*.

Interview with the Vampire (1994)	~~George Fenton~~	Elliot Goldenthal
Sirens (1994)	~~Geoffrey Burgon~~	Rachel Portman
The River Wild (1994)	~~Maurice Jarre~~	Jerry Goldsmith
Waterworld (1995)	~~Mark Isham~~	James N. Howard
The Scarlet Letter (1995)	~~Elmer Bernstein~~	John Barry
Babe (1995)	~~Jerry Goldsmith~~	Nigel Westlake
The Perez Family (1995)	~~Zbigniew Preisner~~	Alan Silvestri
Last Man Standing (1996)	~~Elmer Bernstein~~	Ry Cooder
Marvin's Room (1996)	~~Thomas Newman~~	Rachel Portman
Ransom (1996)	~~Howard Shore~~	James Horner
North Star (1996)	~~John Scott~~	Bruce Rowland
White Squall (1996)	~~James Horner~~	Jeff Rona
Two Days in the Valley (1996)	~~Jerry Goldsmith~~	Anthony Marinelli
Mission: Impossible (1996)	~~Alan Silvestri~~	Danny Elfman
Air Force One (1997)	~~Randy Newman~~	Jerry Goldsmith
Practical Magic (1997)	~~Michael Nyman~~	Alan Silvestri
Breakdown (1998)	~~Basil Poledouris~~	Basil Poledouris[208]
Stepmom (1998)	~~Patrick Doyle~~	John Williams
Les Miserables (1998)	~~Gabriel Yared~~	Basil Poledouris
The 13th Warrior (1999)	~~Graeme Revell~~	Jerry Goldsmith
The Patriot (2000)	~~David Arnold~~	John Williams
The Kid (2000)	~~Jerry Goldsmith~~	Marc Shaiman
Gangs of New York (2002)	~~Elmer Bernstein~~	Howard Shore
Timeline (2003)	~~Jerry Goldsmith~~	Brian Tyler
Troy (2004)	~~Gabriel Yared~~	James Horner

In a few particular cases, despite having a score ready for a movie, the production team ultimately decided to forego music entirely: this happened with *The China Syndrome* (1979; directed by James Bridges), for which no less than two scores were written by Michael Small and Jack Nitzsche (presumably as two separate attempts) but none survived. As we can see from the following short list, Goldsmith was affected by both sides of this phenomenon. It needs to be stated, however, that in the case of *S.P.Y.S.* (1974; directed by Irvin Kershner) and *Legend* (1985), two different scores were used, though in separate distribution contexts. The U.S. release of *S.P.Y.S.* had its own music, while John Scott's score was recorded for distribution outside the U.S.; for *Legend*, the opposite was true:

---

[208] Particular case and as we know, extremely rare: the production rejected the first Basil Poledouris score, but he could rewrite a completely new score. A bootleg edition contains the two Poledouris scores for this movie.

the movie circulated in the U.S. with a score by the German rock band Tangerine Dream, while in the rest of the world it was distributed with Goldsmith's music. The distribution of the best recorded pieces, regardless of whether they were used or not, is nevertheless a very deep-rooted custom, though the (official or unofficial) recordings are not always easy to track down. In the case of Herrmann's *Torn Curtain* and North's *2001*, official recordings of the scores can be found – respectively conducted by Elmer Bernstein and Joel McNeely and by Goldsmith himself. In 1974, Goldsmith wrote the music for *Chinatown* after a different score had been rejected; this rarely happened again, with the exception of *The River Wild* and *The 13th Warrior*.[209] It was more frequent for Goldsmith's own scores to be rejected after having been completed: this happened once in 1988 (*Alien Nation*), twice in 1992 (*Gladiator*, *The Public Eye*), once in 1995 (*Babe*), once in 1996 (*Two Days in the Valley*), once in 2000 (*The Kid*) and once in 2003 (*Timeline*).[210]

---

[209] To these we must add *Seven Days in May* (1964). According to the statements of director John Frankenheimer, Goldsmith was hired after this movie had already been scored by David Amram (who later worked with the same director on *The Manchurian Candidate*, 1962).

[210] *Alien Nation, Gladiator, Two Days in the Valley* and *Timeline*, being complete scores, somehow ended up being included to the 'canon' of Goldsmith's repertoire; the rejection of the *Timeline* score was perhaps the only true mistake, as this score is generally regarded as far superior to the one ultimately chosen for the movie.

Filmography

1957   BLACK PATCH (Allen H.Miller, WARNER BROS.)

1959   CITY OF FEAR (Irving Lerner, COLUMBIA)

1959   FACE OF THE FUGITIVE (Paul Wendkos, COLUMBIA)

1960   STUDS LONIGAN (Irving Lerner, UNITED ARTISTS)

1962   THE CRIMEBUSTERS (Boris Sagal, MGM)

1962   LONELY ARE THE BRAVE (David Miller, UNIVERSAL)

1962   FREUD (John Huston, UNIVERSAL)

1962   THE SPIRAL ROAD (Robert Mulligan, UNIVERSAL)

1963   A GATHERING OF EAGLES (Delbert Mann, UNIVERSAL)

1963   THE STRIPPER (Franklin J. Schaffner, 20TH CENTURY-FOX)

1963   TAKE HER, SHE'S MINE (Henry Koster, 20TH CENTURY-FOX)

1963   SEVEN DAYS IN MAY (John Frankenheimer, PARAMOUNT)

1963   THE LIST OF ADRIAN MESSENGER (John Huston, UNIVERSAL)

1963   THE PRIZE (Mark Robson, MGM)

1963   LILIES OF THE FIELD (Ralph Nelson, UNITED ARTISTS)

1964   GENERAL WITH THE COCKEYED ID (John Sutherland) °°°

1964   SHOCK TREATMENT (Denis Sanders, 20TH CENTURY-FOX)

1964   TO TRAP A SPY (Don Medford, MGM)

1964   RIO CONCHOS (Gordon Douglas, 20TH CENTURY-FOX)

1964   THE SATAN BUG (John Sturges, UNITED ARTISTS)

1964   FATE IS THE HUNTER (Ralph Nelson, 20TH CENTURY-FOX)

1965   MORITURI (Bernhard Wicki, 20TH CENTURY-FOX)

1965   A PATCH OF BLUE (Guy Green, MGM)

1965   THE TROUBLE WITH ANGELS (Ida Lupino, COLUMBIA)

1965   VON RYAN'S EXPRESS (Mark Robson, 20TH CENTURY-FOX)

1965   IN HARM'S WAY (Otto Preminger, PARAMOUNT)

---

[211] Due to lack of space and considering its never-ending evolution, for Goldsmith's discography see: www.jerrygoldsmithonline.com. Some titles currently included in some of the composer's filmographies, such as *The Expendables* (1962), *The Hemingway Play* (1977) and *Dusty* (1983), TV movies, were not confirmed and were therefore cancelled from the list.

1965   THE AGONY AND THE ECSTASY (Carol Reed, 20ᵀᴴ CENTURY-FOX) °
1966   OUR MAN FLINT (Daniel Mann, 20ᵀᴴ CENTURY-FOX)
1966   STAGECOACH (Gordon Douglas, 20ᵀᴴ CENTURY-FOX)
1966   SECONDS (John Frankenheimer, PARAMOUNT)
1966   THE BLUE MAX (John Guillermin, 20ᵀᴴ CENTURY-FOX)
1966   THE SAND PEBBLES (Robert Wise, 20ᵀᴴ CENTURY-FOX)
1967   WARNING SHOT (Buzz Kulik, PARAMOUNT)
1967   IN LIKE FLINT (Gordon Douglas, 20ᵀᴴ CENTURY-FOX)
1967   THE FLIM FLAM MAN (Irvin Kershner, 20ᵀᴴ CENTURY-FOX)
1967   HOUR OF THE GUN (John Sturges, UNITED ARTISTS)
1968   SEBASTIAN (David Greene, PARAMOUNT)
1968   BANDOLERO! (Andrew V. McLaglen, 20ᵀᴴ CENTURY-FOX)
1968   PLANET OF THE APES (F. J. Schaffner, 20ᵀᴴ CENTURY-FOX)
1968   THE DETECTIVE (Gordon Douglas, 20ᵀᴴ CENTURY-FOX)
1968   THE ILLUSTRATED MAN (Jack Smight, WARNER BROS.)
1968   100 RIFLES (Tom Gries, 20ᵀᴴ CENTURY-FOX)
1969   JUSTINE (George Cukor, 20ᵀᴴ CENTURY-FOX)
1969   THE CHAIRMAN (Jack Lee Thompson, 20ᵀᴴ CENTURY-FOX)
1970   PATTON (Franklin J. Schaffner, 20ᵀᴴ CENTURY-FOX)
1970   RIO LOBO (Howard Hawks, NGP)
1970   THE TRAVELING EXECUTIONER (Jack Smight, MGM)
1970   THE BROTHERHOOD OF THE BELL * (Paul Wendkos, CBS/WB)
1970   TORA!TORA!TORA! (Richard Fleischer, 20ᵀᴴ CENTURY-FOX)
1970   THE BALLAD OF CABLE HOGUE (Sam Peckinpah, WARNER)
1971   A STEP OUT OF LINE * (Bernard McEveety, CBS/WB)
1971   WILD ROVERS (Blake Edwards, MGM)
1971   ESCAPE FROM THE PLANET OF THE APES (Don Taylor, 20ᵀᴴ C.-FOX)
1971   THE HOMECOMING: A CHRISTMAS STORY * (Fielder Cook, CBS)
1971   THE CABLE CAR MURDER (Jerry Thorpe, CBS)
1971   CRAWLSPACE * (John Newland, CBS)
1971   THE MEPHISTO WALTZ (Paul Wendkos, 20ᵀᴴ CENTURY-FOX)
1971   THE LAST RUN (Richard Fleischer, MGM)
1971   DO NOT FOLD, SPINDLE OR MUTILATE * (Ted Post, ABC)
1972   SHAMUS (Buzz Kulik, COLUMBIA)

1972   THE MAN (Joseph Sargent, PARAMOUNT)
1972   PURSUIT * (Michael Crichton, ABC)
1972   THE OTHER (Robert Mulligan, 20ᵀᴴ CENTURY-FOX)
1973   THE GOING UP OF DAVID LEV * (James F. Collier, ABC)
1973   ACE ELI AND RODGER OF THE SKIES (Bill Sampson, 20ᵀᴴ C.-FOX)
1973   ONE LITTLE INDIAN (Bernard McEveety, DISNEY)
1973   PAPILLON (Franklin J. Schaffner, ALLIED/WARNER BROS.)
1973   HAWKINS ON MURDER * (Jud Taylor, CBS)
1973   THE DON IS DEAD (Richard Fleischer, UNIVERSAL)
1973   THE RED PONY * (Robert Totten, NBC/UNIVERSAL)
1973   THE POLICE STORY * (William A. Graham, COLUMBIA)
1974   INDICT AND CONVICT * (Boris Sagal, ABC)
1974   S.P.Y.S. (U.S. version; Irvin Kershner, MGM)
1974   A TREE GROWS IN BROOKLYN * (Joseph Hardy, 20ᵀᴴ C.-FOX)
1974   WINTER KILL * (Jud Taylor, ABC/MGM)
1974   HIGH VELOCITY (Remi Kramer, 1ˢᵀ ASIAN)
1974   CHINATOWN (Roman Polanski, PARAMOUNT)
1974   QᴮVII * (Tom Gries, ABC/COLUMBIA)
1975   TAKE A HARD RIDE (Antonio Margheriti, 20ᵀᴴ C.-FOX)
1975   BABE * (Buzz Kulik, CBS/MGM)
1975   RANSOM (Caspar Wrede, 20ᵀᴴ CENTURY-FOX)
1975   A GIRL NAMED SOONER * (Delbert Mann, 20ᵀᴴ CENTURY-FOX)
1975   THE REINCARNATION OF PETER PROUD (J.Lee Thompson, AIP)
1975   MEDICAL STORY * (Gary Nelson, COLUMBIA)
1975   THE WIND AND THE LION (John Milius, MGM)
1975   BREAKHEART PASS (Tom Gries, MGM)
1975   BREAKOUT (Tom Gries, COLUMBIA)
1976   THE LAST HARD MEN (Andrew McLaglen, 20ᵀᴴ C.-FOX) °°°°
1976   THE CASSANDRA CROSSING (G.Pan Cosmatos, AVCO EMBASSY)
1976   LOGAN'S RUN (Michael Anderson, MGM)
1976   THE OMEN (Richard Donner, 20ᵀᴴ CENTURY-FOX)
1976   TWILIGHT'S LAST GLEAMING (Robert Aldrich, ALLIED)
1977   ISLANDS IN THE STREAM (Franklin J. Schaffner, PARAMOUNT)
1977   DAMNATION ALLEY (Jack Smight, 20ᵀᴴ CENTURY-FOX)

1977   MACARTHUR (Joseph Sargent, UNIVERSAL)

1977   COMA (Michael Crichton, MGM)

1977   CONTRACT ON CHERRY STREET * (William A. Graham, COLUMBIA)

1978   DAMIEN: OMEN II (Don Taylor, 20TH CENTURY-FOX)

1978   THE BOYS FROM BRAZIL (Franklin J. Schaffner, 20TH C.-FOX)

1978   THE SWARM (Irwin Allen, WARNER BROS.)

1978   THE FIRST GREAT TRAIN ROBBERY (Michael Crichton, U.ARTISTS)

1978   CAPRICORN ONE (Peter Hyams, WARNER BROS.)

1978   MAGIC (Richard Attenborough, 20TH CENTURY-FOX)

1979   PLAYERS (Anthony Harvey, PARAMOUNT)

1979   ALIEN (Ridley Scott, 20TH CENTURY-FOX)

1979   STAR TREK: THE MOTION PICTURE (Robert Wise, PARAMOUNT)

1980   THE FINAL CONFLICT (Graham Baker, 20TH CENTURY-FOX)

1980   CABOBLANCO (Jack Lee Thompson, AVCO EMBASSY)

1981   THE SALAMANDER (Peter Zinner, ITC)

1981   MASADA: THE HEROIC FORTRESS * (Boris Sagal, ABC/UNIVER-SAL)

1981   NIGHT CROSSING (Delbert Mann, BUENAVISTA [DISNEY])

1981   RAGGEDY MAN (Jack Fisk, UNIVERSAL)

1981   OUTLAND (Peter Hyams, WARNER BROS.)

1981   INCHON (Terence Young, MGM/UNITED ARTISTS)

1982   THE SECRET OF N.I.M.H. (Don Bluth, MGM)

1982   THE CHALLENGE (John Frankenheimer, EMBASSY)

1982   FIRST BLOOD (Ted Kotcheff, TRI STAR)

1982   POLTERGEIST (Tobe Hooper, MGM)

1983   THE LONELY GUY (Arthur Hiller, UNIVERSAL)

1983   TWILIGHT ZONE: THE MOVIE: PROLOGUE & 'TIME OUT' (John Landis, WB.)

1983   TWILIGHT ZONE: THE MOVIE: 'KICK THE CAN' (Steven Spielberg)

1983   TWILIGHT ZONE: THE MOVIE: 'IT'S A GOOD LIFE' (Joe Dante)

1983   TWILIGHT ZONE: THE MOVIE: 'NIGHTMARE AT 20,000 FEET (George Miller)

1983   PSYCHO II (Richard Franklin, UNIVERSAL)

1983   UNDER FIRE (Roger Spottiswoode, ORION)

1984   SUPERGIRL (Jeannot Szwarc, TRI STAR)

1984   GREMLINS (Joe Dante, WARNER BROS.)

1984   RUNAWAY (Michael Crichton, TRI STAR)

1985 BABY: SECRET OF THE LOST LEGEND (Bill W.L. Norton, DISNEY)
1985 RAMBO: FIRST BLOOD PART II (G.Pan Cosmatos, TRI STAR)
1985 KING SOLOMON'S MINES (Jack Lee Thompson, CANNON)
1985 EXPLORERS (Joe Dante, PARAMOUNT)
1985 LEGEND (European version; Ridley Scott, 20TH C.-FOX)
1986 POLTERGEIST II: THE OTHER SIDE (Brian Gibson, MGM)
1986 HOOSIERS (David Anspaugh, HEMDALE)
1986 LINK (Richard Franklin, CANNON)
1987 LIONHEART: THE CHILDREN'S CRUSADE (F. J. Schaffner, ORION)
1987 INNERSPACE (Joe Dante, WARNER BROS.)
1987 EXTREME PREJUDICE (Walter Hill, TRI STAR)
1988 LEVIATHAN (George Pan Cosmatos, MGM/U. ARTISTS)
1988 RENT A COP (Jerry London, KINGS ROAD)
1988 THE 'BURBS (Joe Dante, UNIVERSAL)
1988 CRIMINAL LAW (Martin Campbell, TRI STAR)
1988 RAMBO III (Peter MacDonald, TRI STAR)
1989 WARLOCK (Steve Miner, NEW WORLD)
1989 STAR TREK V: THE FINAL FRONTIER (William Shatner, PARAMOUNT)
1990 THE RUSSIA HOUSE (Fred Schepisi, MGM/PATHE)
1990 GREMLINS II: THE NEW BATCH (Joe Dante, WARNER BROS.)
1990 TOTAL RECALL (Paul Verhoeven, TRI STAR)
1991 NOT WITHOUT MY DAUGHTER (Brian Gilbert, MGM)
1991 MEDICINE MAN (John McTiernan, TOUCHSTONE [DISNEY])
1991 LOVE FIELD (Jonathan Kaplan, ORION)
1991 SLEEPING WITH THE ENEMY (Joseph Ruben, 20TH C.-FOX)
1992 MOM AND DAD SAVE THE WORLD (Greg Beeman, WARNER)
1992 MR.BASEBALL (Fred Schepisi, UNIVERSAL)
1992 MATINÉE (Joe Dante, UNIVERSAL)
1992 BASIC INSTINCT (Paul Verhoeven, CAROLCO)
1992 FOREVER YOUNG (Steve Miner, WARNER BROS.)
1993 RUDY (David Anspaugh, TRI STAR)
1993 SIX DEGREES OF SEPARATION (Fred Schepisi, MGM)
1993 THE VANISHING (George Sluizer, 20TH CENTURY-FOX)
1993 MALICE (Harold Becker, TRI STAR)

1993   DENNIS THE MENACE (Nick Castle, WARNER BROS.)

1994   THE RIVER WILD (Curtis Hanson, UNIVERSAL)

1994   I.Q. (Fred Schepisi, PARAMOUNT)

1994   THE SHADOW (Russell Mulcahy, UNIVERSAL)

1994   BAD GIRLS (Jonathan Kaplan, 20ᵀᴴ CENTURY-FOX)

1994   ANGIE (Martha Coolidge, BUENAVISTA [DISNEY])

1995   POWDER (Victor Salva, BUENAVISTA [DISNEY])

1995   CONGO (Frank Marshall, PARAMOUNT)

1995   FIRST KNIGHT (Jerry Zucker, COLUMBIA)

1995   CITY HALL (Harold Becker, COLUMBIA)

1996   CHAIN REACTION (Andrew Davis, 20ᵀᴴ CENTURY-FOX)

1996   FIERCE CREATURES (Fred Schepisi & Robert Young, UNIVERSAL)

1996   STAR TREK: FIRST CONTACT (Jonathan Frakes, PARAMOUNT) °°

1996   THE GHOST AND THE DARKNESS (Stephen Hopkins, PARAMOUNT)

1996   EXECUTIVE DECISION (Stuart Baird, WARNER BROS.)

1997   L.A. CONFIDENTIAL (Curtis Hanson, WARNER BROS.)

1997   THE EDGE (Lee Tamahori, 20ᵀᴴ CENTURY-FOX)

1997   AIR FORCE ONE (Wolfgang Petersen, COLUMBIA)

1998   DEEP RISING (Stephen Sommers, BUENAVISTA [DISNEY])

1998   MULAN (Tony Bancroft & Barry Cook, DISNEY)

1998   SMALL SOLDIERS (Joe Dante, UNIVERSAL/DREAMWORKS)

1998   STAR TREK: INSURRECTION (Jonathan Frakes, PARAMOUNT)

1998   U.S.MARSHALS (Stuart Baird, WARNER BROS.)

1999   THE MUMMY (Stephen Sommers, UNIVERSAL)

1999   THE HAUNTING (Jan De Bont, DREAMWORKS)

1999   THE 13ᵀᴴ WARRIOR (John McTiernan, TOUCHSTONE [DISNEY])

2000   HOLLOW MAN (Paul Verhoeven, COLUMBIA)

2001   ALONG CAME A SPIDER (Lee Tamahori, PARAMOUNT)

2001   THE LAST CASTLE (Rod Lurie, DREAMWORKS)

2002   THE SUM OF ALL FEARS (Phil Alden Robinson, PARAMOUNT)

2002   STAR TREK: NEMESIS (Stuart Baird, PARAMOUNT)

2003   LOONEY TUNES: BACK IN ACTION (Joe Dante, WARNER BROS.)

°music for the prologue; score composed by Alex North.
°° score co-author: Joel Goldsmith.
°°°° short documentary.
°°°° score actually made by previous Goldsmith music: westerns scores and from the movie Morituri.
* Television movie.

'Rejected scores'

1987 WALL STREET (Oliver Stone, 20ᵀᴴ CENTURY-FOX). Goldsmith probably left the project before writing a single note of the score. The actual composer was Stewart Copeland.

1988 ALIEN NATION (Graham Baker, 20ᵀᴴ CENTURY-FOX). Goldsmith wrote the entire score (available on disc), but it was later replaced by a new score composed by Curt Sobel.

1992 THE PUBLIC EYE (Howard Franklin, UNIVERSAL). Goldsmith wrote the entire score, but it was replaced by a new score composed by Mark Isham.

1992 GLADIATOR (Rowdy Harrington, COLUMBIA). Goldsmith wrote the entire score (available on disc), but it was replaced by a new score composed by Brad Fiedel.

1995 BABE (Chris Noonan, UNIVERSAL). Goldsmith wrote the entire score, but it was replaced by a new score composed by Nigel Westlake.

1996 TWO DAYS IN THE VALLEY (John Herzfeld, MGM). Goldsmith wrote the entire score (available on disc), but it was replaced by a new score composed by Anthony Marinelli.

2000 THE KID (Jon Turteltaub, BUENAVISTA [DISNEY]). Goldsmith wrote the entire score, but it was replaced by a new score composed by Marc Shaiman.

2003 TIMELINE (Richard Donner, PARAMOUNT). Goldsmith wrote the entire score (available on disc), but it was replaced by a new score composed by Brian Tyler.

Minor contributions

1952 DON'T BOTHER TO KNOCK (Roy Ward Baker, 20ᵀᴴ CENTURY-FOX). Goldsmith wrote some additional cues. The actual composer was Lionel Newman.

1965 THE SPY WITH MY FACE (John Newland, MGM). Goldsmith wrote the main theme. The actual score was composed by Morton Stevens.

1967 THE KARATE KILLERS (Barry Shear, MGM). Goldsmith wrote the main theme. The actual score was composed by Gerald Fried.

1991 BROTHERHOOD OF THE GUN (television movie, Vern Gillum, CBS). Goldsmith wrote the main theme. The actual score was composed by Joel Goldsmith.

1995 JUDGE DREDD (Danny Cannon, BUENAVISTA [DISNEY]). Goldsmith only wrote the trailer music; the actual score was composed by Alan Silvestri.

Extra-cinematic works

This list includes the composer's so-called *extra-cinematic works*: this means we chose to gather Goldsmith's concert pieces together with brief cinematic fanfares that can be regarded as "miniatures" for orchestra. The recordings for such works are rare and essentially limited to the two main pieces. Just as we previously did with the composer's movie and TV works, we reported the composition date of each piece and, if known, the name of the musical institution that had commissioned it.

195? TOCCATA FOR SOLO GUITAR

1957 THUNDER OF IMPERIAL NAMES, for band; commission: USAF Command Band.

1961 CINEMA INTERNATIONAL CORP. LOGO

1969 CHRISTUS APOLLO; for speaker, mezzo-soprano, chorus and orchestra, 'Cantata Celebrating the Eighth Day of Creation and the Promise of Ninth', in four parts. Text by Ray Bradbury. California Chamber Symphony. Published by Elcajo Music Company. Goldsmith recalls:

> In 1969, the California Chamber Symphony asked me to write a cantata based on a text by the celebrated author Ray Bradbury. I was thrilled to be asked since I had a relationship with Ray going back to dramatic radio of the 1950s and later the motion picture [1968] *The Illustrated Man* [directed by Jack Smight and produced by Warner Bros.]. The cantata was to be a large piece – orchestra, choir, mezzo-soprano, and narration. Although the text is quite spiritual, I elected to compose the piece using the 12-tone system. I feel there is a great relationship between impressionism and do-

decaphonicism and that was the musical language I wanted for *Christus Apollo*. The piece consists in four parts separated by narration.

1970 A Patch of Blue, ballet (from the music of the 1965 movie); The San Francisco Ballet.

1971 Othello, ballet; National Ballet of Australia.

1972 Music for Orchestra; Saint Louis Symphony Orchestra. Published by Elcajo Music Company. Goldsmith recalls:

> In 1970 I was asked by Leonard Slatkin to compose a short piece for the Saint Louis Symphony. While I was thrilled with the commission, the year was not a good one for me. I was going through a divorce and my mother was seriously ill with cancer. All of my personal turmoil – pain, anger, and sorrow – went into writing *Music for Orchestra* in strict dodecaphonic form. There has been much negative criticism about composing in the 12-tone system, and in today's musical climate, I do think the style is almost anachronistic. But for me [in that period], it was a liberating way to express my deepest feelings. The piece is written in three sections, all based and developed from the same 12-tone row. The first section is quite turbulent, the second introspective, and the third very agitated as it sums up all my feelings in one cathartic release.

1976 Paramount TV Fanfare; commission: Paramount Pictures.

1987 CarolCo Pictures Logo; Carolco Pictures.

1989 Capricorn One, ballet (from the music of the 1978 movie); Ballet Met, Columbus, Ohio.

1993 Cinergi Pictures Logo; Cinergi Pictures.

1996 Universal Pictures Logo; Universal International.

1998 Fanfare for Oscar; Academy of Motion Picture Arts and Sciences.

1999 Fireworks (a Celebration of Los Angeles), for orchestra. Los Angeles Philharmonic Orchestra. Published by Elcajo Music Company. Goldsmith recalls:

> *Fireworks* was composed in 1999 for the finale of my first concert series with the Los Angeles Philharmonic Orchestra at the Hollywood Bowl.

After starting to write what was to be a big extravaganza, I realized that I was writing about the city where I was born and had lived my entire life. I decided instead to make the piece a grand celebration of my childhood, growing years, my years of maturity, and all the events that climaxed with my first appearance at the Hollywood Bowl.[212]

2001 Soarin' over California (Disney California Adventure Theme Park IMAX Ride); Disney. Orchestrations by Mark McKenzie.
2003 C2 Pictures Logo; C2 Pictures.

TV Shows and other television work

Goldsmith's experience in TV shows (or *serials*) and similar products (except for made-for-TV movies, which are listed together with regular movies in the composer's filmography) covers about two decades of intense activity, from the mid-50s' *Studio One* to 1973's *Barnaby Jones*. In later years, the composer's work on television was rather sporadic: Goldsmith scored an episode of *Amazing Stories* in 1986 and wrote the opening credits for a few TV series of the 90s, among which was Emmy Award winner *Star Trek: Voyager* (1995), a piece forecasting Goldsmith's renewed contribution to the *Star Trek* saga. From the late '50s onwards, we can pinpoint the start of the composer's collaborations, as well as the number and title of episodes he contributed to; as for the earlier, mainly anthological series, though their episode titles are shown, there is no exact reference to their date. The two episodes of *Perry Mason* that the composer scored in 1959 are widely regarded as the start of Goldsmith's true TV career. Then came an impressive number of western serials to which he frequently contributed under a pen name (often it was Michael J.Hennagin), composing with the help of orchestrator Arthur Morton. During the first five years of his actual movie experience, therefore, Goldsmith was still busy with a remarkable quantity of tele-

---

[212] The *Christus Apollo*, *Music for Orchestra* and *Fireworks* the composer's impressions can be found in: CD Telarc 80560 cover notes (2002). In this recording, Goldsmith himself conducts the London Symphony Orchestra, with performances by the London Voices, mezzo-soprano Eirian James and, as the speaker in *Christus Apollo*, by the Welsh actor Anthony Hopkins.

vision work. Few of these TV scores were recorded, unfortunately, although the situation has improved in recent years. In at least three separate occasions, moreover, Goldsmith was hired to score a few stand-alone TV specials, including a pilot episode for *Nick Quarry* (1968) a *noir* series that never made it to production.

The following list includes the number and nature of the composer's contribution to TV shows:

1955-56 STUDIO ONE (a.k.a. STUDIO ONE IN HOLLYWOOD) [1948\58, 10 seasons]; Production company: CBS, b/w. Among the directors: Sidney Lumet, Robert Mulligan, Paul Nickell, Daniel Petrie, Franklin J. Schaffner. Music composed, among others, by Bernard Herrmann, Bernhard Kaun, Robert Allen. Goldsmith scored some episodes, including 'The Lovers', 'Silent Flight', 'Old Times', 'Promise', 'Riches', 'Essay', 'Peaceful Soul', 'The Other Place', 'The Lady Died at Midnight', 'The Tongue of Angels' and supervised 'The Left-Handed Welcome' and 'Enemy Within'.

1955 HALLMARK HALL OF FAME [started in 1951]; Production company: NBC (up to 1979), CBS (1979\88), ABC (from 1988); b/w and col. Cast: Lee Vines (speaker), Sarah Churchill, Selena Royle, Dirk Wayne Summers. Among the directors: Maurice Evans, George Schaefer. Cast: Maurice Evans, Jessica Tandy, Judith Anderson. Music composed, among others, by Richard Addinsell. Probably the longest-running anthology series on television. Theatrical TV show; among the authors: Shakespeare, George Bernard Shaw, Charles Dickens, Edmond Rostand, Herman Melville, etc. He scored some episodes.

1955 GENERAL ELECTRIC THEATRE [1953\62; 9 seasons, thirty-minute episodes]; Production company: CBS; b/w. Directors: Anthony Barr, Peter Kortner, Ida Lupino, Leslie H. Martinson, Nicholas Ray; introduced by Ronald Reagan. Music also composed by Elmer Bernstein, Bernard Herrmann, John Williams, Morton Stevens, Fred Steiner. Goldsmith scored episodes 1.38 'Hitler's Secret' (directed by Peter Kortner); 'Last Dance'; 'Sarah's Laughter'; 'My Dark Days'.

1955 CLIMAX! (a.k.a. CLIMAX MYSTERY THEATER) [1954\58; 4 seasons, sixty-minute episodes]; Production company: CBS; b/w. Anthology TV series. Music also composed by Bernard Herrmann. Goldsmith scored some episodes, including 'The Trial of Captain Wirz'.

1955 THE LINEUP (SAN FRANCISCO BEAT) [1954\60; 6 seasons, thirty- and sixty-minute episodes]; Production company: CBS; b/w. Among the directors, Earl Bellamy. Cast: Warner Anderson, Tom Tully, Rachel Ames, Marshall Reed. Music also composed by Bernard Herrmann. Goldsmith wrote the main title music and scored episodes 'Army Armitage' and 'Wake up to terror'.

1956-60 PLAYHOUSE 90 [1956\61, 133 episodes]; Production company: CBS; b/w. Initially a live anthology series, from 1957 it became prerecorded. Among the directors: John Frankenheimer, Arthur Penn, Ralph Nelson, Franklin J. Schaffner. Music also composed by Fred Steiner, Bernard Herrmann, John Williams, Robert Allen. Goldsmith scored episodes 'Requiem for a Heavyweight' (1956); 'Misalliance'; 'A Marriage of Strangers'; 'Dream of Treason'; 'Cruel Day'; 'Rank and File'; 'Shape of the River'; 'Sound of Trumpets'; 'Tomorrow'; 'The Tunnel'; 'Project immortality'; 'Miracle worker' (1957-58); 'Days of wine and roses' (directed by John Frankenheimer).

1957 WAGON TRAIN [a.k.a. MAJOR ADAMS, TRAIL MASTER] [1957\65; 8 seasons, 284 sixty- and ninety-minute episodes]; Production company: NBC/ABC; b/w and col. Genre: western. Cast: Ward Bond, John McIntire, Robert Horton, Dennis Scott Miller. Music also composed by, among others, John Williams. Several main themes, the most famous composed by Jerome Moross. He scored some episodes.

1958 WANTED DEAD OR ALIVE [1958\61; 3 seasons, Pilot and 94 thirty-minute episodes]; Production company: CBS. b/w. Genre: western. Cast: Steve McQueen, Wright King. Main theme composed by Rudy Schrager; music supervision by Herschel Burke Gilbert. He scored some episodes.

1959 PERRY MASON [1957\66; 9 seasons, 271 sixty-minute episodes]; Production company: CBS; b/w. Genre: drama, crime. Cast: Raymond Burr. Main theme composed by Fred Steiner. Goldsmith scored episodes 3.04 'The Case of the Blushing Pearls' (October 24, 1959) and 3.06 'The Case of Paul Drake's Dilemma' (November 14, 1959).

1959 PECK's BAD GIRL [1959\60, one season, thirty-minute episodes]. Production company: CBS; b/w. Cast: Wendell Corey, Ray Ferrell, Patricia McCormack, Marsha Hunt. Music also composed by Wilbur Hatch. He scored some episodes.

1959-60 BLACK SADDLE [1959\62, 3 seasons, thirty-minute episodes]. Production company: NBC/ABC; b/w. Among the directors: Gard Oswald. Cast: Peter Breck, Russell Johnson, Anna-Lisa, Keenan Wynn (narrator). Music composed by Goldsmith with the collaboration of Arthur Morton. Goldsmith used the pen name Michael J. Hennagin, wrote the main title music and, among others, scored episodes 'Client: Travers' and 'End of the Line'.

1959 FOR BETTER OR WORSE [1959\60; thirty-minute episodes]. Production company: CBS; b/w. Among the directors: Dennis Patrick. Cast: Jim Bannon, Dr. James A. Peterson. Music also composed by Bernard Herrmann, Bernhard Kaun, Fred Steiner, Lucien Moraweck. He scored some episodes.

1960-61 FULL CIRCLE [thirty-minute episodes]; Production company: CBS; b/w. Cast: Dyan Cannon, Jean Byron, Robert Fortier, Carter Talton. Music also composed by Franz Waxman, Fred Steiner, Bernhard Kaun, William Grant Still. He scored some episodes.

1960 PETE AND GLADYS [1960\62; 2 seasons; thirty-minute episodes]; Production company: CBS; b/w. Cast: Harry Morgan, Cara Williams, Verna Felton. Music composed also by Wilbur Hatch and Lucien Moraweck. He scored some episodes.

1960-61 THE TWILIGHT ZONE [1959\64; 5 seasons, 156 thirty- and sixty-minute episodes]; Production company: CBS; b/w. Genre: fantasy, thriller. Created by Rod Serling. Among the composers: Marius Constant (who wrote the famous title music from season 2), Bernard Herrmann (also the season 1 main title), Lalo Schifrin, Nathan van Cleave, Fred Steiner. Remake of some original episodes in the 1983 Warner Bros. film *Twilight Zone: The Movie*. Goldsmith scored episodes 1.13 'The Four of Us Are Dying' (directed by John Brahm; January 1st, 1960); 1.27 'The Big Tall Wish' (directed by Ron Winston; April 8, 1960); 1.29 'Nightmare as a Child' (directed by Alvin Ganzer; April 29, 1960); 2.03 'Nervous Man in a Four Dollar Room' (directed by Douglas Heyes; October 14, 1960); 2.12 'Dust' (directed by Heyes; January 6, 1961); 2.13 'Back There' (directed by Heyes; January 13, 1961); 2.15 'The Invaders' (directed by Heyes; January 27, 1961).

1960-66 GUNSMOKE [1955\75; 20 seasons, 635 thirty- and sixty-minute episodes]; Production company: CBS; b/w and Col. Genre: western. Cast: James Arness, Amanda Blake, Dennis Weaver, Burt Reynolds and others. One of the longest TV drama shows in the history of television, not only among westerns. Broadcasted on the radio from 1952, on television from 1955. The main theme was composed by Rex Koury and Glenn Spencer. Goldsmith scored episodes 5.22 'Doc Judge' (February 6, 1960); 6.02 'The Blacksmith' (September 17, 1960); 6.13 'The Wake' (December 10, 1960); 6.20 'Love thy Neighbour' (January 28, 1961); 6.26 'Old Faces' (March 18, 1961); 12.08 'The Whispering Tree' (November 12, 1966).

1960 HAVE GUN, WILL TRAVEL [1957\63; 6 seasons, 225 thirty-minute episodes]; Production company: NBC; b/w. Genre: western. Cast: Richard Boone, Kam Tong, Lisa Lu. This series started on the radio. Goldsmith scored episodes 4.01 'The Fatalist' (September 10, 1960) and 4.03 'A Head of Hair' (September 24, 1960).

1960-61 THRILLER [1960\62; 2 seasons; 67 sixty-minute episodes]; Production company: NBC; b/w. Genre: thriller. Boris Karloff presented and occasionally starred in thriller and horror stories. Several episodes were directed by Ida Lupino. Goldsmith scored episodes 1.15 'The Cheaters' (December 27, 1960); 1.17 'The Poisoner' (January 10, 1961); 1.20 'Hay-Fork and Bill-Hook' (February 7, 1961); 1.23 'Well of Doom' (February 28, 1961); 1.27 'A Late Date' (April 4, 1961); 1.28 'Yours Truly, Jack the Ripper' (April 11, 1961); 1.32 'Mr George' (May 9, 1961); 1.33 'Terror in Teakwood' (May 16, 1961); 1.35 'Dark Legacy' (May 30, 1961); 1.37 'The Grim Reaper' (June 13, 1961); 2.01 'What Beckoning Ghost?' (September 18, 1961); 2.02 'Guillotine' (September 26, 1961); 2.04 'The Weird Tailor' (October 16, 1961); 2.05 'God Grant that She Lye Still' (October 23, 1961); 2.06 'Masquerade' (October 30, 1961). Previously composed music was reused in episodes 2.07 'Last of the Sommervilles' (November 6, 1961) and 2.10 'The Closed Cabinet' (November 27, 1961).

1961 RAWHIDE [1959\65; 8 seasons, 217 sixty-minute episodes]; Production company: CBS; b/w. Genre: western. Cast: Eric Fleming, Clint Eastwood, Steve Raines. Main theme composed by Dmitri Tiomkin. Goldsmith scored episode 3.22 'Incident in the Middle of Nowhere' (April 7, 1961).

1961 DR KILDARE [1961\66; 5 seasons, 132 sixty- and 58 thirty-minute episodes]; Production company: NBC; b/w. Genre: medical, drama. Cast: Richard Chamberlain, Raymond Massey, Jud Taylor, Steven Bell, Lee Kurty. Goldsmith wrote the main theme, which later became the music for the song 'Three stars will shine tonight' sung by Chamberlain. He also scored some episodes.

1961 BEN CASEY [1961\66; 5 seasons; 153 sixty-minute episodes]; Production company: ABC; b/w and col. Genre: medical, drama. Cast: Vince Edwards, Sam Jaffe, Bettye Ackerman, Harry Landers. Main theme composed by David Raksin. The music composed by Goldsmith for a 1965 episode was later used in a *Dr Kildare* episode.

1961-62 CAIN'S HUNDRED [sixty-minute episodes]; Production company: NBC; b/w. Created by Peter Monash. Among the directors: Irvin Kershner; cast: Peter Mark Richman. This TV show is connected to a television movie called *The Crimebusters* (1962; directed by Boris Sagal), which constituted two episodes of the *Cain's Hundred* show. Music composed also by Fred Steiner. Goldsmith wrote the main title music and scored some episodes.

1963 BOB HOPE'S CHRYSLER THEATER (a.k.a. THEATRE OF STARS) [1963\67; anthology series; 53 sixty-minute episodes]; Production company: NBC; b/w and col. Genre: drama, comedy. Presented and produced by Bob Hope. Music also scored by Bernard Herrmann, John Williams, Lalo Schifrin and Benny Carter. He scored some episodes.

1963 KRAFT SUSPENSE THEATRE (a.k.a. THE CRISIS) [anthology series; 59 sixty-minute episodes]. Production company: NBC; col. Genre: mystery. Among the directors, Robert Altman. Music also composed by Bernard Herrmann and John Williams. He scored some episodes.

1964 THE MAN FROM U.N.C.L.E. [1964\68; 5 seasons, 105 sixty-minute episodes]; Production company: NBC; b/w and col.; Genre: action, mystery. Cast: Robert Vaughn, David McCallum, Leo G. Carroll. U.N.C.L.E.: United Network Command for Law and Enforcement. Goldsmith composed the main title music and scored episodes 1.01 Pilot 'The Vulcan Affair' (directed by Don Medford; September 22, 1964); 1.05 'The Deadly Games Affair' (directed by Alvin Ganzer; October 20, 1964); 1.13 – 'The King of Knaves Affair' (directed by Michael O'Herliny; December 22, 1964). In *The Girl from U.N.C.L.E.* (1966/67) the main title theme was reused in a new musical arrangement.

1965 VOYAGE TO THE BOTTOM OF THE SEA [1964\68; 4 seasons, 110 sixty-minute episodes]; Production company: ABC; b/w and col. Genre: adventure. Created by Irwin Allen. Cast: Richard Basehart, David Hedison, Robert Dowdell, Terry Becker. Goldsmith scored episode 2.01 'Jonah and the Whale' (directed by Nathan Juran; September 19, 1965). The music for this episode was later reused in a different episode.

1965 THE LONER [1965, one season, 26 thirty-minute episodes]; Production company: CBS; b/w. Genre: western. Cast: Lloyd Bridges. Created by Rod

Serling. Goldsmith's main theme for this show was inspired by the *Lonely Are the Brave* theme, a 1962 Universal production. Alexander Courage scored some episodes. Goldsmith scored episodes 'An Echo of Bugles' (directed by Alex March) and 'One of the Wounded' (directed by Paul Henried).

1965 THE LEGEND OF JESSE JAMES [one season, 35 thirty-minute episodes]; Production company: ABC; b/w. Genre: western. Created by Samuel A.Peeples. Cast: Chris Jones, Allen Case, Ann Doran. Donald Siegel directed some episodes. He scored some episodes.

1966 JERICHO [1966\67; one season, 16 sixty-minute episodes]; Production company: CBS; col. Genre: war, mystery. Cast: Don Francks, John Leyton, Marino Mase. Lalo Schifrin composed the main theme. He scored some episodes.

1968 NICK QUARRY [Demo for a TV show, 15 minutes long]; Production company: 20th Century-Fox.; col. Genre: noir, crime story. Directed by Walter Grauman. Cast: Tony Scotti, Gena Rowlands.

1969 ROOM 222 [1969\74, 5 seasons, 113 thirty-minute episodes]. Production company: ABC; col. Created by James L.Brooks. Cast: Lloyd Haines, Denise Nicholas, Michael Constantine, Karen Valentine. Among the directors: John Erman, Leslie H. Martinson. Music also composed by Benny Golson. Goldsmith composed the main title music and scored the pilot and some of the other episodes.

1972 LIGHTS OUT. Production company: CBS; col. Special: 'When Widows Weep', sixty minutes (January 15, 1972). Pilot for a never produced TV series, based on the eponymous live show on air from 1946 to 1952.

1972 THE WALTONS [1972\81; 9 seasons, 221 sixty-minute episodes]; Production company: CBS/NBC; col.; Genre: drama. Cast: Richard Thomas, Judy Norton, Eric Scott, Mary Elisabeth McDonough. Music composed also by Arthur Morton and Alexander Courage. Goldsmith composed the main title theme and music for episodes 1.01 (September 14, 1972 – 'The

Foundling'); 1.05 (October 12, 1972 – 'The Typewriter'); 1.06 (October 19, 1972 – 'The Star'); 1.09 (November 09, 1972 – 'The Ceremony'); 1.11 (November 30, 1972 – 'The Literary Man'); 1.13 (December 14, 1972 – 'The Reunion'). Goldsmith also scored the television movie *The Homecoming: A Christmas Story*, directed by Fielder Cook (December 19, 1971).

1972 ANNA AND THE KING [one season, 13 thirty-minute episodes]; Production company: CBS; col. Cast. Yul Brinner, Samantha Eggar. Richard Shores also scored some episodes.

1973 HAWKINS [1973\74; one season: pilot and 7 ninety-minute episodes]; Production company: CBS; col. Genre: drama, mystery. Cast: James Stewart, Bonnie Bedelia. Goldsmith composed the main theme and scored the television movie 'Hawkins on Murder' (a.k.a. 'Death and the Maiden', 1974, directed by Jud Taylor), the pilot of this show. Among the composers, George Romanis scored two episodes, Jerry Fielding three, and Jeff Alexander two.

1973 BARNABY JONES [1973\80; 8 seasons, 178 sixty-minute episodes]; Production company: CBS; col.; Genre: detective story. Cast: Buddy Ebsen. Goldsmith composed the main title theme and scored the pilot episode 'Requiem for a Son' (January 28, 1973).

1973-74 POLICE STORY [1973\80; 5 seasons, two-hours Pilot and 96 sixty-minute episodes; plus a few more occasional episodes up to 1988]; Production company: NBC/ABC.; col. Genre: action, crime. Among the directors: John Badham. Music also composed by Richard Markowitz. Goldsmith wrote the main theme and scored episodes: Pilot 'Slow Boy' (September 20, 1973); 1.06 'Collision Course' (November 20, 1973); 1.07 'Death of Credit' (November 27, 1973); 1.08 'The Big Walk' (December 4, 1973); 1.11 'Chain of Command' (January 8, 1974); 1.16 'Country Boy' (February 19, 1974); 1.20 'Chief' (March 19, 1974). Goldsmith also composed the music for the television movie *The Police Story* (1973), directed by William A. Graham.

1974 POLICE WOMAN [1974\78; 4 seasons, Pilot e 92 sixty-minute episodes]. Production company: NBC; col. Genre: detective story. It's a *Police Story* spin off. Cast: Angie Dickinson. He scored some episodes.

1975 ARCHER [1975; one season, 6 sixty-minute episodes]; Production company: NBC; col. Cast: Brian Keith, John T.Ryan. Goldsmith created the main theme and scored the episode 1.04 'Shades of Blue' (February 20, 1975).

1975 ADAMS OF EAGLE LAKE [1975; 2 sixty-minute episodes]; Production company: ABC; col. Based on the television movie *Winter Kill* (1974). Cast: Andy Griffith. Goldsmith composed the music for the original movie, later re-used in episodes 1.01 (January 10, 1975) and 1.02 (February 26, 1975).

1975-76 MEDICAL STORY [1975\76, one season, 13 sixty-minute episodes]. Production company: NBC; col. Genre: medical. Cast: Tony Musante, Meredith Baxter. Goldsmith composed the main title theme and scored the pilot and some other episodes.

1986 AMAZING STORIES [1985\87; 2 seasons, 45 thirty-minute episodes]; Production company: NBC; Col. Produced by Steven Spielberg. Main theme composed by John Williams. Music also composed, among others, by Danny Elfman and Michael Kamen. Goldsmith scored episode 1.17 'Boo!' (directed by Joe Dante; February 16, 1986), starring Bruce Davison and Andrea Marcovicci.

1990 H.E.L.P. [one season, 6 sixty-minute episodes]; Production company: ABC; col.; genre: adventure. Directed by Michael Ray Rhodes and E.W. Swackhamer. Cast: Tom Bresnahan, David Caruso, Wesley Snipes. Goldsmith's son, Joel, scored some episodes; he composed the main title music.

1995 STAR TREK: VOYAGER [1995\2001; 7 seasons, 172 sixty-minutes episodes]; Production company: UPN; col. Genre: science fiction. Cast: Kate Mulgrew, Robert Picardo. Goldsmith composed the main title music. The score was actually composed, among others, by Dennis McCarthy, Jay Chattaway, David Bell and Paul Baillargeon. Also in *Star Trek: The Next Generation* (1987-94), Goldsmith was the author of the main title music, although it was an adaptation of the main theme (the 'Enterprise Theme') from *Star Trek: The Motion Picture* (1979).

Radio work

Goldsmith's first experiences in musical application occurred in radio. Between 1950 and 1958 the composer contributed to simple anthological or dramatic radio shows (not unlike the beginning of his later TV experience). His exposure to this typical "training ground" is little documented, and direct references to single episodes of each radio show are rare and incomplete. We can, however, assume that the composer's contribution was fairly regular. We thus reported the documented shows, specifying whether Goldsmith also happened to write the music for a program's opening and closing credits.

1950-54 ESCAPE [about 240 episodes on air from July 7, 1947 to September 25, 1954]; Radio drama western. Production company: CBS. In 1954 replaced by *Gunsmoke*. He scored some episodes.

195? JUVENILE COURT. Goldsmith composed the main title music.

1953-55 HALLMARK HALL OF FAME [1953\55, 72 episodes]. Biographical drama series. Production company: CBS. Goldsmith scored some episodes. On television from 1951 to 1979, mainly produced by NBC.

1955 ROMANCE [1947\57, about 280 episodes]. Production company: CBS. Goldsmith scored episodes 'Autumn Love' (unknown date); 'Last Summer Love' (July 9, 1955); 'The Sergeant and the Lady' (unknown date).

1956 SUSPENSE [945 episodes on air from June 17, 1942 to September 30, 1962]. Radio drama thriller; Production company: CBS. Goldsmith scored episode No.669 'The Strange Prophecy of Bertha Abbott' (October 16,

1956); cast: Sam Edwards, Richard Crenna, Ann Doud.

1957 THE CBS RADIO WORKSHOP [85 episodes on air from January 27, 1956 to September 22, 1957]. Production company: CBS. Goldsmith scored episode '1489 Words' (February 10, 1957).

1958 FRONTIER GENTLEMAN [41 episodes on air from January 29 to November 16, 1958]. Radio drama western; Production company: CBS. Goldsmith composed the main title and closing title music.

BIBLIOGRAPHY/VIDEOGRAPHY

Film music and 20th century music essays

-Sergio Bassetti, *La musica secondo Kubrick*, Turin, Lindau, 2002.

-Jeff Bond, *The Music of Star Trek*, Lone Eagle, Los Angeles, 1999.

-Cristina Cano e Giorgio Cremonini, *Cinema e musica- il racconto per sovrapposizioni*, Florence, Vallecchi, 1995.

-Michel Chion, *La musique au cinéma*, Paris, Fayard, 1998.

-Ermanno Comuzio, *Colonna sonora: dizionario ragionato dei musicisti cinematografici*, Rome, Ente dello Spettacolo, 1992. 2nd edition: *Musicisti per lo schermo*, ibid., 2004 (2 vol. including cd-rom).

-Sergio Miceli, *Musica e cinema nella cultura del Novecento*, Florence, Sansoni, 2000.

-David Morgan: *Knowing the Score*, New York, Harper Collins, 2000.

-Christopher Palmer, *The Composer in Hollywood*, London/New York, Marion Boyars, 1990.

-Roy M. Prendergast, *Film Music: a Neglected Art*, New York/London, W.W.Norton & Company, 1992 (1st edition: 1977).

-Tony Thomas, *Music for the Movies*, Los Angeles, Silman-James, 1997 (1st edition: 1973).

-Garrett Bowles, 'Ernst Krenek', in Stanley Sadie and John Tyrrell (ed.), *New Grove Dictionary of Music and Musicians*, London, Macmillan, 2001, vol.13, p.895-899.

-Graham Bruce, *Bernard Herrmann: Film Music and Narrative*, Ann Arbor, UMI Research Press, 1985.

-Malcolm S. Cole, 'Eric Zeisl', in *New Grove, op.cit.,* vol.27, p.772.

-Armando Gentilucci, *Guida all'ascolto della musica contemporanea*, Milan, Feltrinelli, 1992 (1st edition: 1969).

-Cosimo Malorgio, *Censure di un musicista: la vicenda artistica e umana di Mario Castelnuovo-Tedesco,* Milan, Paravia, 2001.

-James Methuen-Campbell, 'Jakob Gimpel', in *New Grove, op.cit.,* vol.9, p.874.

-Sergio Miceli, *Morricone, la musica, il cinema*, Milan/Modena, Ricordi-Mucchi, 1994.

-Roberto Pugliese, *Bernard Herrmann*, Venice, Circuito Cinema, 1982.

-Id., *Miklós Rózsa*, Venice, Circuito Cinema, 1982.

-Miklós Rózsa, *A Double Life- A Spelling Autobiography of Success and Survival in*

the Golden Age of Hollywood, New York, Wynwood, 1989².
-STEVEN C. SMITH, *A Heart at Fire's Center- The Life and Music of Bernard Herrmann*, Berkeley, University of California Press, 2002.
-JAMES WESTBY, '*Mario Castelnuovo-Tedesco*', in *New Grove*, vol.5, p.255-258.

Essays, articles and interviews in film music magazines
Various articles from "Film Score Monthly" (United States); "Music from the Movies" (Bristol, U.K.); "Soundtrack! - The Collector's Quarterly" (Mechelen, Belgium).

Filmographies and discographies of Jerry Goldsmith
-RONALD L. BOHN, ALLAN BRYCE, JAMES MACMILLAN, LUC VAN DE VEN, DANIEL MANGODT, *A filmography/Discography of Jerry Goldsmith*, in "Soundtrack!", vol.12 n.47, September 1993, p.22-42.
-LUC VAN DE VEN, *Jerry Goldsmith Filmography, part 1 – 1993-1999*, in "Soundtrack!", vol.18 n.69, Spring 1999, p.40-42.
-ID., *Jerry Goldsmith Filmography, part 2 – Recent Releases (referring to Films & Television Scored 1959-1993)*, in "Soundtrack!", vol.18 n.69, Spring 1999, p.43-45.

Audiovisual material (DVD's)
-*Alien*, 20th Century-Fox Home Entert., F4 01090, 2000. Isolated score by Goldsmith.
-*L.A.Confidential*, Warner Bros, Z8 14913, 1997. Isolated soundtrack (music by Goldsmith and songs by various artists).
-*The Omen Trilogy, 25th anniversary edition*, 3 DVD's, 20th Century-Fox Home Entertainment, F4 08976.1-3, 2001. Contains *The Omen, Damien-Omen II, The Final Conflict*; brief Goldsmith interview about *The Omen* music.
-*Planet of the Apes*, 20th Century-Fox Home Entertainment (35th anniversary edition), 2003. Audio running commentary by the composer.
-*Poltergeist*, Warner Bros Z8 50165, 2000.
-*Star Trek: The Motion Picture: Director's Edition*, 2 DVDs, Paramount Pictures, Pds 20041, 2000. Audio running commentary by Goldsmith, director Robert Wise and others.
-*Hollow Man*, Columbia Pictures, Dc 24020, 2001. Audio running commentary by Goldsmith and isolated score.

***

Acknowledgments

This edition is the translation of my book *Jerry Goldsmith e la musica nel cinema americano*, published by Robin Edizioni, Rome, 2012. My acknowledgment goes to: Professor Giovanni Guanti, to whom I am deeply thankful, and my family. Special thanks to my friend and translator Cecilia Martini.

This book is dedicated to the memory of my cousin Paolo and of my fellow University student and friend Francesco Attanasi.

37471185R00096

Made in the USA
Lexington, KY
04 December 2014